Also by George Kalamaras

POETRY BOOKS
Luminous in the Owl's Rib (2019)
That Moment of Wept (2018)
The Hermit's Way of Being Human (2015)
Kingdom of Throat-Stuck Luck (2011)
The Recumbent Galaxy (2010)
(with Alvaro Cardona-Hine)
Gold Carp Jack Fruit Mirrors (2008)
Even the Java Sparrows Call Your Hair (2004)
Borders My Bent Toward (2003)
The Theory and Function of Mangoes (2000)

POETRY CHAPBOOKS
The Mining Camps of the Mouth (2012)
Symposium on the Body's Left Side (2011)
Your Own Ox-Head Mask as Proof (2010)
Something Beautiful Is Always Wearing the Trees (2009)
(with paintings by Alvaro Cardona-Hine)
The Scathering Sound (2009)
Beneath the Breath (1988)
Heart Without End (1986)

POETRY SPOKEN WORD CD
A Thousand Thousand Fireflies Never Equal Zero (2013)
(with Omowale-Kétu Oladuwa and Michael F. Patterson)

CRITICAL STUDY
*Reclaiming the Tacit Dimension: Symbolic Form
in the Rhetoric of Silence* (1994)

WE SLEPT THE ANIMAL

Letters from the American West

GEORGE KALAMARAS

DOS MADRES

2021

DOS MADRES PRESS, INC.
P.O. Box 294, Loveland, Ohio 45140
www.dosmadres.com   editor@dosmadres.com

Dos Madres is dedicated to the belief that the small press is essential to the vitality of contemporary literature as a carrier of the new voice, as well as the older, sometimes forgotten voices of the past. And in an ever more virtual world, to the creation of fine books pleasing to the eye and hand.

Dos Madres is named in honor of Vera Murphy and Libbie Hughes, the "Dos Madres" whose contributions have made this press possible.

Dos Madres Press, Inc. is an Ohio Not For Profit Corporation and a 501 (c) (3) qualified public charity. Contributions are tax deductible.

Executive Editor: Robert J. Murphy

Book Design: Elizabeth H. Murphy
www.illusionstudios.net

Author photo: Jim Whitcraft
Cover art: Alvaro Cardona-Hine, "Masked Ball" (35" x 37"),
reproduced with the kind permission of Barbara McCauley
(of the Cardona-Hine Gallery)

Typeset in Adobe Garamond Pro, Copperplate & Chaparral Pro
ISBN 978-1-953252-08-1
Library of Congress Control Number: 2020946775

First Edition
Copyright 2021 George Kalamaras
All rights reserved. No part of this book may be reproduced or transmitted in any form or by any means graphic, electronic or mechanical, including photocopying, recording, taping or by any information storage or retrieval system, without the permission in writing from the publisher.
Published by Dos Madres Press, Inc.

ACKNOWLEDGMENTS

I want to thank the editors of the following magazines in which most of these poems, or their previous versions, first appeared:

Atticus Review: "Below Buffalo Willows," "Dejected in Boulder, I Think of James Wright's 'Depressed by a Book of Bad Poetry, I Walk Toward an Unused Pasture and Invite the Insects to Join Me,'" "Letter to Megan from Rifle," "Letter to Patrick from Fort Collins," and "Letter to Sue from Durango"

Calibanonline: "Letter to Jim [Harrison] from Rifle," "Letter to John [Olson] from Denver," "Letter to John [Tritica] from Ouray," "Letter to Judy from Colorado Springs," "Letter to Larry from Bellvue," "Letter to Paul from Timnath," "Letter to Reg from Cheyenne," "Little Infinite Poem, Or Letter to Bob from Everywhere at Once," and "*Snow on the Backs of Animals*. Letter to Dan from Centennial"

Cloud Rodeo: "Letter to Jay from Boulder" and "Letter to Tom from Stove Prairie"

Copper Nickel: "Belating the Butchered Herd" and "Colorado Sheep Wars, 1894" (both poems finalists for the 2011 *Copper Nickel* Poetry Award)

Court Green: "Letter to Hugo from Nowhere," "Letter to Nate from Steamboat Springs," "Letter to Robert from Ridgway," "Letter to Tony from Cheyenne Wells," "Letter to Tremblay from Tie Siding," and "Saidshaft. Letter to Mary [Rising Higgins] from Albuquerque"

CutBank: "Letter to John [Haines] I Neglected to Send, So Am Finally Sending Now, Twenty-Two Years Late," "Letter to Hugo from Cowdry," and "*What Thou Lovest Well*. Letter to Hugo from Big Timber"

Cutthroat, A Journal of the Arts: "House of Green Buffalo Hides. Slabs of Hump at Right, North Montana, January 1882" (finalist for the 2011 Joy Harjo Poetry Award)

Dispatches from the Poetry Wars: "Letter to Kent from Fort Wayne"

The Drunken Boat: "Dead Skunk," "Letter to Ray from Livermore," and "Letter to Roger from Gunnison"

Fifth Wednesday: "Letter to Marie from Fort Garland"

Flatirons Literary Review: "Letter to John [Zimmerman] from Bellvue"

Four Way Review: "Letter to Phil [Appleman] from Manitou Springs"

From the Edge of the Prairie: "Letter to Forrest from Laramie" and "Letter to Sam from Crow Agency"

Ghost Town: "Letter to Andrew from Livingston" and "Letter to Noah from Castle Rock"

Malpaís Review: "I'm Writing Gene a Letter," "Letter to Alvaro from San Luis," and "Letter to Arthur from Ault"

Map Points: "Letter to Don from Gunbarrel" and "Letter to Eric from Cripple Creek"

Talisman: "Letter to Gerrit from Aurora" and "Letter to Michelle from Victor"

I am also grateful to the following for reprinting poems:

CutBank: "Letter to Gerrit from Aurora," "Letter to Judy from Colorado Springs," "Letter to Tremblay from Tie Siding," and "*Snow on the Backs of Animals*. Letter to Dan from Centennial"

Litscapes: Collected Writings 2015 (Steerage Press): "Letter to Don from Gunbarrel"

Malpaís Review: "Colorado Sheep Wars, 1894," "Dejected in Boulder, I Think of James Wright's 'Depressed by a Book of Bad Poetry, I Walk Toward an Unused Pasture and Invite the Insects to Join Me,'" "Letter to Judy from Colorado Springs," and "Saidshaft. Letter to Mary [Rising Higgins] from Albuquerque"

Thanks, as well, to New Michigan Press for selecting and publishing a chapbook, *The Mining Camps of the Mouth*, as winner of the 2012 New Michigan Press/*DIAGRAM* Chapbook Award, in which a few of these poems previously appeared.

"Letter to the Mikautadze Dance Troupe from Livermore" appeared as a limited edition broadside from Mudra Press.

I want to thank Indiana University-Purdue University Fort Wayne for a 2011 Summer Faculty Research Grant and the Indiana Arts Commission for a 2011 Individual Artist's Fellowship—both of which provided essential time and support to work on this book.

Finally, I want to thank all my friends and cohorts who have always been there for me as brothers and sisters in what Gary Snyder calls "the real work"—many of whom I embrace with a letter in this book. Very special thanks to John Bradley, who read these poems one at a time as I sent them over the loping rails of our letters. Special thanks, as well, to Barry Maxwell (a former editor of the long-standing Montana journal, *CutBank*), who generously encouraged this project, recognizing my deeper intent with these letters—to bring attention to the gifts of each of those to whom I've written. No words can express my thanks to my wife, Mary Ann Cain, for what we share in love and work. And—of course—I offer deep gratitude to Richard Hugo; although we never met or corresponded, his life and poetry (especially his book, *31 Letters and 13 Dreams*) provided the blueprint for this book.

TABLE OF CONTENTS

THE HOW AND WHY THEY DIED

Colorado Sheep Wars, 1894 — 1

ALL THE WORDS WE HAVE BOUND AND GAGGED

Letter to Juan from North Platte — 5
Letter to Joe from Durango — 8
Letter to Robert from Ridgway — 10
Letter to Phil [Appleman] from Manitou Springs — 12
Letter to Arthur from Ault — 14
Letter to Bill [Ryan] from Wellington — 17
Letter to Patrick from Fort Collins — 18
Letter to Tom from Stove Prairie — 22
Letter to Don from Gunbarrel — 24
Letter to Hugo from Nowhere — 26

HOUSE OF GREEN BUFFALO HIDES

House of Green Buffalo Hides. Slabs of Hump at
 Right, North Montana, January 1882 — 31

THE HOBBLE-SOUND OF NOW

Letter to John [Haines] I Neglected to Send, So Am Finally
 Sending Now, Twenty-Two Years Late — 37
Letter to Judy from Colorado Springs — 41
Letter to Ray from Livermore — 43
Letter to Nate from Steamboat Springs — 45
Letter to Mary [Crow] from the Snow of Buffalo Bones
 on the Laramie Plains — 48
Letter to Reg from Cheyenne — 51

Letter to Eric from Cripple Creek — 53
Letter to John [Olson] from Denver — 56
Letter to Larry from Bellvue — 58
What Thou Lovest Well. Letter to Hugo from Big Timber — 61

BELATING THE BUTCHERED HERD

Belating the Butchered Herd — 67

GOOD LONG ANIMAL LUCK OF BEING ALIVE

Letter to Marie from Fort Garland — 75
Letter to Jim [Harrison] from Rifle — 77
Snow on the Backs of Animals. Letter to Dan from Centennial — 80
Letter to Andrew from Livingston — 82
Letter to Alvaro from San Luis — 84
Letter to Tremblay from Tie Siding — 88
Letter to Sam from Crow Agency — 91
Letter to Megan from Rifle — 94
The Branch Will Not Break. Letter to Kevin from Livermore — 97
Letter to Hugo from Cowdry — 100

ZEBRA HIDE OF THE HEART

Dead Skunk — 105

LITTLE INFINITE POEM

Letter to Bill [Stafford] from Fort Collins
 (Just Back from Polson) — 109
Little Infinite Poem, Or Letter to Bob
 from Everywhere at Once — 111
Letter to Sue from Durango — 115
Letter to Roger from Gunnison — 119
Letter to Lisa from the In-Between — 122

Letter to John [Zimmerman] from Bellvue — 124
Letter to Jim [Grabill] from Boulder — 127
Letter to Gerrit from Aurora — 128
Letter to John [Tritica] from Ouray — 130
Letter to Tony from Cheyenne Wells — 133
Letter to Hugo from Kicking Horse Reservoir — 136

ALL THE PATIENCE OF BROTH

Dejected in Boulder, I Think of James Wright's "Depressed by a Book of Bad Poetry, I Walk Toward an Unused Pasture and Invite the Insects to Join Me" — 141

THE BRAHMS-BITTEN. THE SWEET

Letter to Forrest from Laramie — 145
Letter to the Mikautadze Dance Troupe from Livermore — 147
Letter to Noah from Castle Rock — 150
Letter to Jay from Boulder — 152
Letter to Phil [Woods] from Red Feather Lakes — 154
Letter to Michelle from Victor — 156
Letter to Paul from Timnath — 160
Letter to Kent from Fort Wayne — 162
Saidshaft. Letter to Mary [Rising Higgins] from Albuquerque — 166
I'm Writing Gene a Letter — 168

WE SLEPT THE ANIMAL

Below Buffalo Willows — 173

Notes — 175
About the Author — 181

for John Bradley—

*who has no letter in this book
but to whom every letter here is also written*

*Pray hard to weather, that lone surviving god,
that in some sudden wisdom we surrender.*
—Richard Hugo

*For the first time I understand
I'm an animal too.*
—Tom Hennen

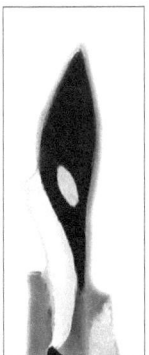

THE HOW AND WHY THEY DIED

Colorado Sheep Wars, 1894

> "*Thirty-eight hundred sheep were stampeded [by angry cattlemen] over a bluff into Parachute Creek on September 10th while their owners were at the Peach Day celebration in Grand Junction. . . . A posse from Parachute found a mass of dead sheep at the foot of a thousand-foot bluff . . .*"
> —*Craig Courier*, September 14, 1894

The how and why they died. The pleading eye. The I can't forget. They couldn't talk. Walk. True north in Colorado is how they ate the lush of it and died. The Bear River Valley and all that sad. The how and why I cry. All southern Wyoming-wide. Something keeps mashing, keeps smashing me with cloven hooves and wool. No, jumping off a cliff is not cliché. Stampeding, less so. Anything we do is dread weight. Wait here, I'd say. And I'd get down on all fours and swim the river-sog into my fleece. No, they couldn't walk. Ticks clung to their swim. Stones to under their hoof. Hooves. We must cross. We must cross our mouths out with stones. Cobble together our fierce. The distance between *here* and *here* is always *there*. Show me your arm's length, and I'll demonstrate beautiful human demise. Of all the animals of Parachute Creek, they are dead and most dying. Alive. Like words. The Union Pacific coupling cars on the track. Laramie and back. Stampeding the mouth's scar.

Brandish the Circle K. Say it's for *Craig* or *Courier* or the *cursive cut of something wrong*. Carve my heart out with soap. The wash the wool the rain across the plains. Tell me the newsprint is strong. That unlike the herd, it can talk. Hear. That the café. That Cheyenne. That the hostess with the bad tattoo will shiver me a bowl of stew. We are marked with many scars. She with me, I with her desire for *my* desire to save the world with a word. The hungry of it and quick. Her shoulder that carries the sad. We might our mouths. Not coals cut hot in woolly flesh or grass. Not the horizontal pupil in the eye. The bah bah bawling of before and beautiful. No, never the wide of the eye. *Forgive us their death*, I'd say, directly into the buzz of a botfly. How to jump off a cliff and survive. The size of all things said. Sad. Of the secret war of how the grass was won. Of death driving death off a bluff forever into the pounding mouth of now.

ALL THE WORDS WE HAVE
BOUND AND GAGGED

Letter to Juan from North Platte
for Juan Felipe Herrera and Ray Gonzalez

We'd slept in that day a quarter century
ago. Weekend reunion at Ray Gonzalez's
pad. Ray in his bed, you on the futon, me
in my sleeping bag on the living room
floor. When you woke and saw me
cocooned with my sleep mask
still on, you both laughed and called me
Zorro! And I parried back, groggily,
still weighted with mud grains
of sleep, saying, *Yes, that's right;
I'm just catching my cosmic Zzzs.*

Then we sloshed coffee and listened
to all our favorite jams: Santana's
Caravanserai. Peter Green. Derek and the Dominos'
"Got to Get Better in a Little While." Jimi's
"Catfish Blues," where he wailed that he wished
he was a catfish, Lord, way down in the pond scum scrum.

What muddy sea did we dive into, Juan? What cloudy
depths? You christened us the Catfish Butterfinger Band
that day. We swam through the guitars, sunk
into their riffs, then surfaced afterwards,
reading the poems of Neruda, Vallejo, and Whitman.

I ain't no catfish, Juan, but I'm now in an ocean
of prairie grass here in North Platte, poised
to cross into Colorado. Not the clichéd kind—
waves of grass and bending wheat—but a turbulent,

churning bottom. Migrant workers here
abound. Soybeans. Broom-corn. Sugar beets. So much
of the world has changed. So much,
the same. We wander here to there, lifetime to lifetime,
doing our work, as if on the backs of those magnificent cranes
an hour west in the sandhills of Ogallala. Do we fly
in their celestial wake? Do we land, biting the night air
for mayflies on the backs of our flock? Sink
our wobbly, stick-figure legs into what we can
never quite see? Or do we grow a lugubrious mustache
like confounded catfish aching through rain, mud-scouring
pond scum for any lost particle of love?

A quarter century ago we were together. LaGrange,
Illinois, where Ray lived in what he called
LaStrange. So few people of color
that when we drove that day to Denny's for brunch,
patrons stopped mid-bite and stared
at you and Ray. We could have stepped right out
of the Fillmore, the warm-up band
for Jimi—welcoming back 1970. I told myself,
Forgive them, for they know not
what music we have brought through their door,
the humming chemistry of love
we all carry inside us.

Ah, how we ignored them, as we ate egg
skillets with potatoes, onions, and melted cheese.
Seasoned, yes, with Tabasco and jokes,
with the copper mines of Neruda,

with Vallejo's *exuberant political need
to love*. We've loved one another a long time, Juan,
in the ache and age of this city or that. There is no
barrier to our friendship, no "big, beautiful wall."
And Mexico is certainly not paying
for any of it. The sister with the shopping cart
and all-night tarp on Fullerton
is paying. The mother who works a third job night shift
at Wal-Mart is paying. The brother coughing his guts
out onto a rag he uses for a hanky.

Mid-fork they stared, in a town that was,
indeed, *LaStrange*. We, the Catfish Butterfinger Band,
mining the muddy depths, pumping the discarded grit
and gravel of the world in and out of the breathing
of our breeding poems. Down below, in mounds
of Lorca's ants, his arsenic lobster
still threatens to rise, then crash down upon our heads
both blessings and rebuke. As we scour for food in what is
most dark. With Jimi and Carlos. With Clapton still imploring,
"Got to Get Better in a Little While." With Pablo,
César, and Walt. With pine winds praising
the hinge of the world, whingeing it both ways
at once. As we sat there twenty-five years ago
with our eggs. With poems memorizing
our mouths. As we sit—still—with our eggs and the promise
of birth. Waiting—we, the Catfish Butterfinger Band.
With Pablo—for the copper miners to emerge
from their caves. With César—to perforate the pores
of the world with his *exuberant political need
to love*. With Walt—for the sleepers to awake.

Letter to Joe from Durango
for Joseph Gastiger

All the Durango dead, Joe. All the *poetry* dead. Railroad yards
empty, even with carloads of metal from nearby Silverton

to Denver. Somehow we survive in twos. You and me. Ritsos
and Seferis. Even your crossed shaman toes at birth.

Magritte said, *This is not a pipe*, but George Seferis smoked
his, becoming "Mathios Paskalis Among the Roses." Then

a mermaid manifested from his chest, onto a ship
where she was *crucified to the wheel while she was still*

beautiful. There is crucifixion of the poor. Daily.
And there are platitudes hanging from the Judas Tree

for thirty pieces of silver. Yes, silver was torn from these hills
to build this town of gunfights, boardwalks, and saloons.

I remember meeting in the great in-between. 1980.
Fort Collins. Your going-away party. Me just arriving

in Colorado from Indiana. You leaving the next morning
for DeKalb, Illinois. Say the map of the U.S. over your kitchen

table that evening showed more than I-80 from here to there.
Say it was two or more ways of mouth. Say it showed how

connected we were, even in our unknowing as we moved
on the same path as two reflecting moons. Coltrane said,

I start in the middle of a sentence and move both directions at once.
Seferis was Mathios Paskalis and George Seferis together.

As if the living dropped among the Durango dead.
The Silver Bill Repeal made way for gold. Yet our coins

continued to be minted in both. Once, you swore Williams'
triadic line paralleled his breathing following his stroke.

We breathe through one another, Joe, as if a possum
and a tree, though we often go months without words.

I know you as the sun-drenched moon. The moon-drenched
swamp. Like lightning guttering the throat during an afternoon

storm in Durango. Trains need two tracks, with switchbacks
to sycamore the hills. We use both nostrils to breathe the lost

particles of gandy-dancer dust. I could be one hundred
and still be dead inside if they vowed to burn the communist

love poems of Ritsos. You and I favor the rain inside a couplet
because one drop can marry another. Imagine a night sky

as if the furthest constellation curved inside our own
left ear. Imagine that map above your table platting

not just rivers but the words we'd one day speak.

Letter to Robert from Ridgway

for Robert Kelly

I have all but six of your eighty-eight books, Robert. This is not self-praise but to say I am still somehow wanting. Last night, throughout sleep, I held a young woman thirty years, though I am forty-one years happy with my wife. Her name was Larissa, the same name as Yuri Zhivago's lover. I do not exaggerate, nor can I ignore the fact that *Yuri*, in Russian, means *harmonic ground*. We are in love with a primitive sadness. With all we can possibly regret? Schenkel said, *Submission is the effort of the inferior to attain friendly or harmonious social integration*. Wolves are not people, outside of some magical moment in Grimm's. They are certainly not books of poems with many words lined against one another, spines sun-bleached, as if hens' teeth in the belly of a whale. I could work with questionnaires. I could ask you in multiple ways how much weeping entered your poems and where. Ridgway resembles the Himalayas. Cross your leg and meditate on *these* mountains. What strikes me most are names with texture like Telluride, Ouray, and Ridgway. Some perfectly female name for *fox* or *henhouse* or *underground entrance to the sacred domain of seeds of green peppers*. Rarely, if ever, delegations of eye contact sophisticate our hearing. The way you looked at me, tenderly, seventeen years ago, insisting you sign every book of yours on my shelf. It took you at least an hour. For this reason, I have remained undead.

The altitude in Ridgway is so high, the air thins the membrane between this world and the other. Could Whitman's late-life circumcision be said to have opened his heart? Could it have removed the final barrier, in that incarnation, between self and world? You are praying to Milarepa. To Padmasambhava. My students, to strange abbreviations on *Facebook*, *Instagram*, and *Twitter*. Last week, they wondered at the weeping I refrained as I read them the long closing section of "The Sleepers." I sometimes float slantwise through this animal throat and that in the electrical fields of sleep. Through the broad-breasted possibility of women who might love me. Even a woman the age of the rain. Like last night's Larissa. Aggression toward elephants and submission toward rats? Forgiveness is a storm weathering another day of sun? To be so briefly male and then at the final moment become a piece of perfect music? Cravings in the blood confuse me. Couplings come in many forms—for many incarnations—from chocolate, to Silver Needle white tea, to even a hound dog napping on my lap. One morning when Rumi departed for errands, his teacher, Shams, took all his sacred books and sank them thirty feet in a well. How many species of dust mites did you lose when you dropped all that weight? What have you left behind each morning on your meditation mat, in my house when you bowed that evening before my altar photos of yogis? It is like a thing of great innocence to count slowly from one to eighty-eight, pausing to pass a finger over the spine's fatigue, to worry all the words we have bound and gagged.

Letter to Phil from Manitou Springs
for Philip Appleman

Did Darwin name the world, or did you, Phil,
in creating him for us? I swear a Galápagos tortoise
inhabits my sleep. A dream broth. A cup
of Genmaicha tea containing roasted grains
of brown rice. It lays its eggs across the coral reef
of my brain. Blonde. Blind. Without fish-mouth
or salt. The three readings for the day
from the Church of Francis Ponge would most certainly
be "The Oyster," "The Mollusk," and "Abode
of the Gray Shrimp." What am I looking for here
in Manitou? Perhaps the primordial pulse
of the manta ray let loose through fossils
of an ancient mountain pass. Imagine the ragged shore
of the Baltic Sea and a big black wolf in 1835
that we believed was the other side
of the world. Imagine Apollo, patron of shepherds,
associated with wolves—though only out of fear
of certain parts of ourselves that might never die.
We kill hundreds of thousands of breaths,
regularly, when we breathe mindlessly,
without focus. A shaman in Siberia
shakes his maraca, reaching into me, and holds my liver
right there in a basket before me, telling how
to track my past. How my mouth might finally be
the beautiful, brutal slaughter of 4,000 geese
in the spring hunt off Cape Krestovskaya.

Your poems are more beautiful than the Crimean dead,
than the Japanese glaze of a soap dish waiting

to cleanse my mouth in the Manitou Crafts Co-op.
I still remember your class. 1978. How J and I
noticed the sweet peculiarity of your blue suede
shoes. Did they evolve from the bellowing blast
of yak leather? From the low vocabulary in the underbelly
of an ox? How many people know that the musk ox
is more closely related to the North American
mountain goat than to the bison? How much chocolate
can one possibly eat in this tranquil tourist town
of Manitou without vomiting a goldfish, forcibly,
all the way down from the watery restlessness
of the brain? I keep returning to Stevens
because I don't understand, though I love the sound
of his verbs. *Come. Go. Stay. Be well*, he seems to say.
Even when sounding like the rarely glimpsed
freshwater mountain shrimp of Borneo. Once,
when writing about Vallejo, I quoted Stevens by mistake,
saying, *the ordinary of his commonplace*. Once,
writing you, I asked if you were a mirror
of the purest milk, my most moist lice, or just
my mouth, thirty years older than the rest of me.

Letter to Arthur from Ault

for Arthur Sze

Things happen at once. Crocodile farms in Australia harvest
hatchlings of "problem" crocs warm in December. Santa Fe's

money can't thwart the sudden influx of drugs. Hoodlums
up from Albuquerque. Bikers from Española. You in India.

In Santa Fe. Imagine a dog-day harvestfly. The membrane
on either side of its abdomen vibrating one of the loudest

sounds any insect can make. In common parlance, we call this
death. We name it *music*. We say, *Mr. and Mrs. Square*

will never allow their son to marry the daughter of a Circle.
Look at the Banaras rudraksha beads in your hand. Look

at the Santa Fe town plaza where they sell jewelry
every afternoon at three. It has four sides that go round

and round? I bought a green turquoise bolo at Dressman's
eighteen years ago because it reminded me of 1956

when my parents were born unto me. Such pests as lice
and bedbugs have devolved to lose their wings. Grape Beetle.

Figeater. Goldsmith Beetle. Cloaked Knotty-Horn. There is
some speculation that coyote pups start howling

because of *the outcome of pleasure they find in making a noise.*
I'm in Ault, Arthur. There is no noise. Farm-post.

On the edge. Of everything. The only noise here is farming
combines. One good breakfast joint with too much bacon fat.

Last coffee before the Pawnee Buttes. My house in Livermore
no longer on fire, as if a perfect future. One coyote begins.

Immediately two or more join in. Yes, there are poems
from the T'ang Dynasty still making the rounds of collective

composition. Tu Fu keeps saying, *And the war goes on and on.*
Li Ho's mother repeats, *My son will not stop until he has vomited*

up his heart! Meng Chiao fails his government exam again
and again. You're in Banaras. The wheel slowly turning. You

and Carol and Sarah stepping onto the very rickshaw
Mary Ann and I rode through monsoon many summers

before. The imprint of our ghost-bodies welcoming you. No,
you're back in Santa Fe, dry this year. Navajo vendors

completing three sides of a square? Ault, I tell you,
ought to be outlawed. One of those places where Roethke

recruits Hugo, Kizer, and Wright to sling it out with him
once and for all against the Earps. The outcome of pleasure

they find just in making a noise. One poem pulsing in the dust,
oozing out of a torn left word. A stanza scowling down,

twirling a blur of spurs. Sun-glint, unshaven, cruel, across
stubbled syllables at noon. Something in the in-between.

In the gaps. In the spaces between people spectating the street.
Listen to a harvestfly's abdomen grating a sound. To a coyote

pack, coming on at dusk, joining in. For good long luck.
For the twilight plight. In the east and west of our own

mouths. Just to make a noise. Together. To belong.

Letter to Bill from Wellington

for William Ryan

How many hurricanes   how many wind-rips, Bill,
have to hit us   hard   until we   awaken
unto the grit and gulfs of the world?   The bullfrogs   the
sparrows   a snowy owl too far   south
that somehow got confused   fossilized and
underground   flaring up   through us   the way
wind carves names   into us,   names
like Ault or   Pueblo or   Wellington, Colorado. Even
Monroe, Louisiana.   You're several hundred miles
south and east.   In the wind in the   rain,

and I'm standing in the buffalo   remains
of a dry   lakebed   in Wellington
where you once lived many animals   ago,
serving whiskey   rounds   at The Duke
to the not-quite-dead.   The Poudre Canyon,
the foothills.   On fire.   And I'm wondering where
the water went   where the cool   pools
when the rain fails   and the fires come.

When the fires come,   all the animals drop
down   into us and become   us. Become   the aged
ache, the world we were   and went   and will be
     again. The ash and tug   and toughening
turns   of our   tongues.

Letter to Patrick from Fort Collins
for Patrick Lawler

Morning headlines confide, *Anchor Breaks Down*
    Over Verdict, Anniston Flaunts Bikini Bod,
        Beckham Shows Baby Bump, Snake Born

with Two Heads. I don't know where to burn
    first. Toward a woman crying out for touch?
        Or inside, where a different cry resides?

Mary Ann's in the store, Bootsie and me parked,
    cottonwood-cool, on the nap. I keep massaging my
        joints, knowing you're in there too. You grew

up in a basement, Patrick. People laugh, think it a joke.
    But you had no house. After school you'd approach
        a slab, descend cement into all that lack

of electricity. *Why can't we. Live in a house. Like everybody.*
    Else. Family took your mouth. Mangled my tongue.
        Took us both dumb. I'm writing from Fort

Collins, down the Livermore mountain for food.
    The horse neighing me awake, says, *Appaloosa appalls*
        even the mall, says, *Palomino is more than a motel*

on the north end of town. For a long time
    we have been brothers in how to survive.
        You below ground, me above. 7,600 feet

higher than you in Liverpool. New York
    hurt-holds raw as sugar ripped from the rib
        of an owl metabolizing mice into a rush

of blood-orange. Makes me hope Mary Ann returns
    with apples. One a day keeps the throat. Words
        stick in the long way down. Their intent,

sharp as all we hold back. There's a young blonde
    with gorgeous denimed hips and two armloads
        of food, screaming at a little dawdling boy.

I know her word comes onto him, *in*,
    like the goo of deranged crustaceans.
        He wants to sink through the parking lot

into the ocean of blurred word where
    he can forever and again the strands
        of her hand. He's missing something.

He's incomplete. It's not a verb. It's not his
    mother's hair. He's only five and wants
        to grow up and leave his monkey bars,

live in a basement where the light can't
    leach. *What did you do at night?* I asked.
        Simple, you said. *When the sun went down,*

we went to bed. It takes a long time
    for the sun in Fort Collins to die,
        as if the sky were equally shy. I consider

the bikini bods and baby bumps of life,
    that two-headed snake. Remember
        the three-headed Hydra of our past. Father,

son, and holy smoke that smothered us
    both. Let me make my mouth. Let me
        exact your stance. Your Irish father

who loved to drink. His eldest son.
    A basement whose house had ashed-
        over white. We all take our time.

We all try dying. We are all children
    of divorce. Even if *we* is *me*.
        We this and that, we yes and

no, we anchor or steam. All the way
    down through dichotomous dust.
        We one word less, each word

broken, chousing after thin-ribbed calves,
    cowpoke-slow. Let us step our ponies
        over fallen timber. Let us palomino

and pinto and bay. Some people are secretly
    trees when the light goes off, breathing in
        bed through knotted backs aching weight,

leaking all that pine resin as we stand wind-stiff
    tough. Me, in the log-cut of Livermore. You,
        in upstate New York, no boyhood door,

pulling a shower curtain across a pole to say
          goodnight. We survive. Somehow
                    I arrive when Mary Ann emerges

with the pears and enough coffee
          for two, and the blonde with the hips
                    and the jeans and her scolding

is gone. We this and that, we fallen
          log, we dichotomous and dust—
                    Mary Ann and me, your past and mine,

the word *live* pine-lodged in Liverpool.
          In Livermore. Thirty-three miles back, we
                    climb 2,600 feet above Fort Collins. We try

what it was like for you but in reverse. We cry
          out. Descend the steps. Even as we
                    climb. Each day and sink. Into,

away from, our youth. This rise. In elevation.

Letter to Tom from Stove Prairie
for Tom Delaney

Even a little rain can hurt. Sheep scab, for example, is caused by a microscopic mite whose entire life cycle—from emergence from the egg to laying its own—is only three or four days long. We come into this life, Tom, with many scars. It is enough that the world comes in fragments upon the eye. A group of horses, say, might surround us in a pasture with both a lumbering forgiveness and a bad case of croup.

Clear the throat. Cough a goldfish fin back out onto the hanky.

Coffee at The Junction forty years ago, and now we agree: making love with a weeping willow is not optimum. Let me remind you that cycles of procreation are inexact. The Wyoming toad is believed to have inhabited the Laramie Basin since the last ice age. And now, only 100 adult toads remain in the state.

Among famous Wyoming horses, Dapple Dan—the gorgeous gray from Company C—was the only army survivor of the Fetterman Fight near Fort Phil Kearny in western Nebraska. The window of breathing can be narrow. Our gallop and its lather—the hard-pound ground—only a hatchet-sway away.

Sheep, they say, can only be dipped safely three or four months a year.

I see ewes in Stove Prairie, consider bands of them north near the Big Horns, their coats peeling in chunks, exposing vulnerable underbellies. Their miserable scratching against an outcrop—even against each other—spreading the disease.

Still, they continue to graze, Tom, uphill rather than down. The way words bump into one another. All the years we could have been but weren't. Our breathing. Forty years in the aching.

Letter to Don from Gunbarrel
for Don Byrd

Just five or six ant turds up the road from Boulder,
Don. This town's name can fill a person with buckshot.
Jackrabbits damage crops so bad that in the West
they'd been rounded up and driven into pens
for slaughter. The long bones in a bat's wing
correspond to bones in our arm, hand, and fingers—
the thumb is short and ends in a claw. I won't say it
was a dream. It was all so green. Green the dark. Green
the hills. So green the Gunbarrel graves stayed gray.
There's a veterinarian here whose office is connected
to a taxidermy. Remember, Wallace Stevens placed a jar
in Tennessee. Duncan taught a summer
just five or six ant turds from here. His mother
was a falconress. And he was your teacher. And you,
mine. Do this simple equation of pain:
$1 + 2 + 3 = 0$. My mother, too, was a falconress. Here,
remove my hood and tiny jangling bells. In the marsupial
possum, only thirteen embryos can possibly survive,
one for each magical teat in the warm of the pouch's
calm. Try dislodging the tiny things with nail polish
remover, and you smother your own dark
sound. Crickets have been known to eat paper,
cotton, linen, furs, even rubber. Paramecia
are slipper-shaped protozoa, covered with hairlike cilia
that move at the rate of ten to seventeen beats
a second. Still, we can't see enough to measure them
except with a special scope. On the other hand,
among the other significant unsolved problems
is the development of human genitalia. In Boulder,

genitals count, especially among the beautiful
young. Gorgeous sway of this hip and that.
And how fast we age. When it rains, a certain fish
up the canyon gets its name. If Stevens loved chaos,
order courted Williams. I do not say this lightly,
but I have a taste for thirteen ways to eat Don Byrd stew.
Some wingèd thing mounted on the knotty pine
wall, which had muffled my mother's wrist? A clinic
and a taxidermy? We aren't already whole, even when stuffed
with lice? One civilization is always rubbing up against
the next. One species of healing and display. Count
the ant turds it takes to get from here to there.
Somehow, we didn't get hurt.

Letter to Hugo from Nowhere

It was the animal testicle you ate that spring
when the herds swayed down from Glacier.
It brought you something low-slung through bunchgrass.
First, the snows thawed like a man without a drink,
all night with no ride and only the sweats.
Then inside storms found rain could never heal.
I want to say it right, even if I might
miss your grave with an occasional twelve-beat line.
Form, I've heard, equals content. We want order. We crave.
Trains couple on the track. We're frayed, already
stuck in our words like dogs swollen
into each other. They know no other
way. They whine. Howl. They're nowhere,
and so am I, mending snow-fence against weight.

Something is always wet and drift. That part
of me frozen in the hunched shoulder.
I thought my life would be a shame. Thoreau.
Emerson. Times with books I want to die. We
were kids together, Dick, you and I. Decades
and now death separate us. I'm sorry.
You never meant to hurt. You hurt me
with your poems, even where they healed. How could
anyone with such pain refuse death in the face?
We need a name, strong and belligerent,
fleeing north with the war party like Rain-in-the-Face.
They say he got the name when in a fight
in his youth his cheeks were streaked with Cheyenne
blood. We need a word against the massacre
of our mouths, a gone-wrong to stand our strength

against sorrows of the entire whirl
whipping us from Wilsall to Clyde Park and all
the way to Ringling. This is no circus.
We speak hoops of fire the tigers take.
Roar and pace, and somehow we leap through.
Our words, serious as strife and girth.
The lives we've died to get here are real. Ask
Emerson who read the Upanishads.
Ask Thoreau how many lives it takes just to
become human. And still he stroked a locust tree
as if hosts of honey tippled inside the leaves.

We might forget the bees until the stinging
comes. Till it sings. Sometimes in pleasure.
Sometimes in death. We tremble and sweat and shake
we never met. We'll one day meet, I swear,
even if I write a poem as if you spoke
from absolutely nowhere, as if I bought
your life back with stalks of cheatgrass. A poem
about something's nothing, though that nothing
is never absolute. The ten-beat line
might give it shape, drive, and not from the beating
hand of your grandmother angry with guttural rain.

When will you be reborn? Where? Will your mother
keep you this time, even if unwed? How
can I find? You are nowhere and still
steering your Buick from frown to frown,
whipping the wheel from Missoula through wide
river valleys to Choteau, Montana.
Even here in Colorado, you carve

me down from the ranches of Livermore
to Fort Collins where I first read your words
from *Kicking Horse* as I sat at Horsetooth
Reservoir and imagined I was you.
It was the animal. You ate the way
it bled from the neck. You ate the way
it fled from people pushing from behind.
Angry spurs and angry ways, a Philco
in White Center toward which you had to strain
to hear jazz when grandparents went to bed
at eight. A later ache in Deer Lodge or Butte
when you tuned your car to weather, static
pop and snap in the vast in-between. First
the snows, then the thaw, then sheets and sheets
of impossible mountain rain. Sink, now,
into sound ground.

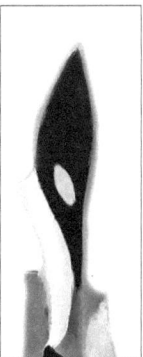

HOUSE OF GREEN BUFFALO HIDES

House of Green Buffalo Hides. Slabs of Hump at Right, North Montana, January 1882

based on a photograph by L.A. Huffman

> "*The hunter usually shot the first buffalo through the lungs so that it would bleed and totter for a little while before it dropped. The others nearby would then become curious and smell or hook the wounded animal, thus concentrating their attention on the victim and not on the source of the danger.*"
> —Mark H. Brown and W.R. Felton

1.
A sitting position with rest sticks
was preferred by most,
two to three hundred yards downwind
of what would die. *Make the kill
in as small an area as possible*, he had said,
as if discourse might serve to distance death itself.

2.
I'm writing a letter to a possum,
begging it to remain dark to the day.
Come out only at night, I plead. Emerge
through the pores of women
who wash the sheets of Denver and hang them
out on lines to moisten the not-yet-sunken moon.

3.
Judging from his notes, the photographer
seemed to love the great woolly beasts.
*I got a lump in my throat each time the pick-axe
was slid into the hump of the not-yet-dead.*
Then, on page thirty-eight, in the margins, a scribble:
Bring little Samuel a green hide as a memento.

4.
I put the book down and begged of it and clutched.
I walked thirty-three feet into the moon
that somehow bled back broken plates of sorrow.
Yes, it was the full moon over Livermore, bathing
the Laramie Plains. But it was also the killing
moon over Dodge. The abalone moon over Abilene.

5.
Still writing the possum, I corrected
the untanned salutation to say, Dear *Opossum*.
Then I finished dressing the rest of the letter
before it lost its winter rode, *I am living in the Ohouse of the Ogreen
Buffalo Hides. Nothing is Ogreen here in this Ohouse.
It is just a little washout Oroofed-in with Ogreen-green hides.*

6.
How might a word my mouth?
How might what's missing most miss?
How, why, and in what way are we to belief, believe, begin?
For how long and for whom do we remain untreated?
Yes, it was the full moon over Livermore, bathing my brain,
but also the blistering moon over Big Timber. Over mine tailings in Butte.

7.
When the wolfer arrived with his strychnine
and traps, the Breaks of the Missouri
seemed to widen, as if the earth itself was tearing apart.
Buttes. Draws. The buffalo hunter responded by bringing: one cook
stove with pipe; three wall tents; one saddle horse and three wagons;
three sheets of patch paper; and thirty Wilson skinning knives.

8.
Dear watery wing of the owl.
Graze my save and my knoll.
Grant me the safe of nightly speak.
Possum my mouth with *this* penance and *that*.
Blink thy sacred eye, like a human—upper lid
down—not like other birds that mark the world in reverse.

9.
A kneeling position with armrests
was preferred by those who prayed.
Make the kill in as small an area as possible,
they whispered to no one in particular, burrowing into the incision
point in the heart. Eliminate all darkness. Journey there only
at night, like any nocturnal beast, in search of voles, mice, mites.

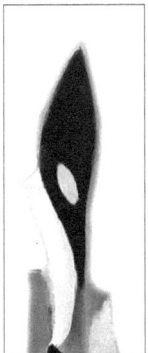

THE HOBBLE-SOUND OF NOW

Letter to John I Neglected to Send, So Am Finally Sending Now, Twenty-Two Years Late

for John Haines

That's no working dog, George,
you chuckle, my beagle-hound
lounging on my lap. You telling me

about your dog team and hauling wood
through snow several months deep,
stopping to skin a moose

before another storm. The afternoon light
of Helena is particularly amber. You slug
a bit of whiskey, a bottle of Jim Beam

on an old cottonwood stump
between us, and ask about Indiana and hounds
and my wife and me not having ever had

children. It is 1998. Our summer in a cabin
in Montana. No phone, no email, nothing
except General Delivery in Big Timber.

I remember the winter of '47, you tell me.
*In the long dark. Alone. Reading Tu Fu snowy
nights by kerosene lamp. Wandering*

*the great northern territories
with him. In exile.* I remember Indiana,
John. My own lantern nights. The moon

milking the sycamores. Lamplight
of 1961 still flickering inside, making me
want the quiet of hickories, maples,

and elms. Those woods I keep
walking further into, in the dark
of midnight light. Took us till the 90s

to meet. And I tell you how your books made me
snow inside. Ran lynx tracks
and hare traps near streams that converged

in my heart. The throaty growl
of your and Joy's German Shepherd
scares all twenty-six pounds of my hound

into sniffing every aching board
of your floor. I'd put my nose down,
too, if I sensed being saved

by what's below. So we separate the dogs
and bring my hound outside
to her royal seat, again, on my lap. You repeat,

That's no working dog. Tender
for a forest tough, for a woodsman
who salvaged wood for his cabin

from an old bridge over Gasoline Creek,
laying trapline from Norfolk, Virginia,
to Vallejo, California, into desire

for the frozen north, for western light leaking through
cottonwoods here in Helena. All afternoon we talk
and hold Indiana and Alaska together like fraternal twins

in the liminal space of Montana. I think of Tu Fu,
how that first winter you must have worried
your hair white as his, worried with him

that the kerosene might not hold
till the thaw. That the fellowship you sought
in exile might leave you both

lonely as lemmings limping toward
the Bering Sea. So we embrace
goodbye. Not in Fairbanks

or Fort Wayne, but somewhere
in-between. Now, I see
there's a letter from you, John,

unanswered, that I've kept as a totem
twenty-two years on my desk. Makes me
remember the things you were

comfortable enough to ask. As you sloshed
the amber back-burn from a bottle
you brought all the way

from Milepost 68. And the moon rose
that evening in Indiana and Alaska, Montana
and somehow as far west as Hunan Province

all at once. The solitude
of Tu Fu ruinous and round
in the great white waves

of *both* of our veins, a moon washing
the sycamores full and warming
our throats. I won't say I'm sad;

I refuse regret. Your unanswered letter
waits for me to be and not be
who I am, who we could *both* become

when our words, traveling the Tanana River
or the Wabash, might flow into a common stream
below a cutbank, braid through

one another, and—again—finally meet.

Letter to Judy from Colorado Springs
for Judith Johnson

This is the city of Nikola Tesla—how all that electricity could have been here and ignored. Buried in shafts. Released. I could spend lifetimes and never understand how a person could kill, claiming God, from lightning strikes on Pikes Peak to radium in the healing waters of Colorado and Manitou Springs. I hate the hotels. The bagels are boring. Part of me would rather giveth my human fur unto the muleskinners and the traps. Let me thank you, my darling, for the birds of prey overhead, for the hawk you sent decades before, keening through my gut. You called it by baby bird names. You called it Whitman and salt. Bachelard and phosphorous. Even Marie Ponsot and a cure for consumption. I never breathed so well as I do now. I never knew you in Belgium. Nor the uranium implanted in your once-twenty-eight-year-old throat. I never knew how in almost dying you could so clearly reach twenty-three years ahead into my grief. When they eat dirt, I understand, earthworms are not merely feeding but are also digging a burrow. I could have spent decades longer as a hermit, before meeting you, content to carry a hut in my throat-latch thatch, and Whitman would have never discovered the line's great ache, the dislocation of Long Island gnats in Conestogas in the Missouri Breaks. Was it you or Bachelard who slept all those years in the same bed with his idiot brother? How can I sleep with myself and allow my invisible woman body to make me more of a man?

What can I finally bring you? Gift you? How shall I tell? When do we love *without* love? The death of the mother-mouth is all it takes for a rain curtain to fall, fiercely from the West. *It is necessary*, it is written, *to be necessary*. Given the expression of *the thin-gummed man*, there is so much we continue to hide. You once wrote of a *great angry owl in search of its kill*. You visited this place years before, though it was Aspen, writing poems with Paul Blackburn and becoming more of the world. There are *cities of mathematics* and cities of sleep. *A poetics of generosity*. What happens to the soul when the breath breaks apart into phosphorus and zinc? Mine tailings of raw religion have claimed this place from generations of Cheyenne. Have stripped it in a frighteningly ancient way—fish by fish, fossil by fossil—from there to here. The imprint of the shy octopus in the rock can still bite—mixing poison in its saliva—and pull one's diving mask off, dragging something almost human to the bottom of even *these* mountains. Oceans of prairie grass not that far east are not a cliché when one speaks of even one bone of the buffalo dead. Yes, I say *buffalo*, not *bison*. It is sometimes good to not be too precise. For the gush of gold, Judy. For the pour of ore that—with the Silver Bill Repeal—ached this place. For the sake of something more. We prayeth this city of Tesla, complete, return us unto the pores of the tongue—divine and electric, replete.

Letter to Ray from Livermore
for Ray Gonzalez

Hey Ray. We know Breton and Desnos are dead,
though not in our poems. I was thinking today
how we love the West. The *real* West where railroads
speak. Everything now is air. Rush here, fast there.
Our molecules jiggle enough as it is
when we microwave our food. That baked potato
I ate last night still striving inside me to survive.
Of course you'll visit in July and sleep
with your head to the north, aligning yourself
with the pines. You remember growing up
on the border with scorpions, the desert
and its sting. I recall Indiana fire ants
in the pump-house ivy. My boyhood
bites. John says they're in my wrist.
And I believe him, standing some nights as I do
like the guy in *Un Chien Andalou*, staring
at my hand. I know. The wrist is not my hand,
but like those railroad tracks, our veins keep wending
west. Each year for me from Fort Wayne to Livermore.
I don't know, sometimes, how we've survived this long
with a moth wing for a mouth. Something is beating me
back, and I'm sure it's me. Part fly, part sky. You named it
Luna and started a magazine. You got the night
just right. I've gone inside, my eye open to the spiritual
fly. Buzz here. Land there. Let the breath
and with it the jittery monkey mind release.
It's surprising we still have wives, the way our parents left
one another with pain. We're not unique. Someone
is always throwing someone out, even with a word

or curve of earth. Someone is always throwing
a bone to the dog. In your case, cats. Remember
when Punk and Whitey loved to eat cantaloupe,
as far back as Arvada? God, we've known each other
a long time, even before them, in Denver,
knowing what makes our secret strain
exact. When Desnos sleep-talked, he threw a thread
of speak that wound from the cosmic now into the lives
of human dread. That's why they were scared
and barred him from the group. So there are strains
of purpose and strains of pain. Which brings me
to how you and I do. Which brings me back
to those two rails running west
and all the courage of the plains. Of course,
Richard Hugo could be a sap. And he knew it.
But he stands naked, letting the wind. Like blood
into a cup, it pours out his mouth. And the trees
speak. Not only booze, dark bars, and shame,
but the hope of how to survive in Red Lodge,
Missoula, or Butte. Desnos knew this
too, stumbling back from the camp, typhus
bleeding his skin, swelling
his spine, the Second World War
pouring out through his teeth. As did Breton,
by the time he got to his third wife. I love them most
for their blurring and slurring of word. The how and why
my life. As we love Hugo too, perhaps most
for his shame in how the West was won
and keeps losing itself in the lost. Because living here
is pine-dead hard. The how and why we cry.

Letter to Nate from Steamboat Springs
   for Nathaniel Mackey

So, the owl peopled our pupils   with hurt   healing
light.   So, we considered the animal-dead
and made them   a bed of most earnest breathing.

There were journeys to the Congo and from. From this. From
that.   Even bats   commanded from the tamarind
to the body   of Baba Kina Ram,   all the way from
sixteenth-century India, carved inexplicable caves.   The
Andoumboulou,   you said,   are our steepest craves.
Cliff-faced. Rock. Failed   humans. The cock crowing
three rhymes   through muslin   to wrap the never-really
dead. We descend   into the breath-kiva   even as we
climb? Snake holes   where the dark dens-up
into sight?   Steamboat Springs, Nate. Steam from a pot
of Genmaicha   tea. Spring from fall.   Winter
from summer.   All the seasons collide
where weather, wet,   goes gold.

Somehow   knew it. Somehow   placed what was put.
Someone placed the bone   from a ham steak on a plate
and gave it an eye.   The eye   of God   or of
René Magritte?   The eye of the owl   or its
meticulous mice   craving death's excess. Of words,
           we have them
and   don't.   We have so little to offer
the mountain lions in Livermore   except clichés about
death and breaths caressed. Bears   populating Steamboat

                    as if all the fur   of the world.
As if   we could all be saved and   not
made   into a rug.

Belovèd friend. Marvelous   mother-tongue   stung
in the silent of all   the crying out. Place an abstraction
anywhere in the word.   Place it   into the concrete
slab   beneath a home   about to be
built from buffalo. Robes and bone   are what sustain,
even among tourists in shorts and   too-tight t-shirts
in Steamboat Springs.   Women are curved.
The men,   fat. Bellies protruding   all the pounding
ground   of cattle   in their flee.

Yesterday, the rattlesnake on the gravel road,   run-over
by the truck in front,   looked at me moments
before death, seeming to say,   *Brother, help me.* I won't.
Tell you   how later I cried.   How the cries,
full-mooned and bloomed,   of coyotes seemed lonelier than
alone. I don't want to   die but live a life of pure animal
                                sung.
Yes, they speak the skeletal unction   of bone.
Anoint the remains of   words passing   through
the digestive tract.   No, they don't say.   Human words
can hurt or   heal. Human tongue. *Anything* human, I say,
can somehow   and   almost.

Or might not?   In Steamboat,   down the steep
from Rabbit Ears Pass, we can hear. If we choose
India's gong. The cleansing gauze   unrolling

down   the yogic throat. All the bodily wrongs.
          Of Banaras. Of
the Congo.   Dogon   dos and don'ts. Of the ancient
sway of Mali.   Of the   thrumming
drum.   Or—further down—of the Andoumboulou
underground. We can choose a ham steak   or a hambone,
milking the marrow   where all the mice might
thrive.   Because   you have sung. Because
the bees begun. Because we have sing or singe or bolus
burnt of almost-human   thought. Because the nouns go
wrong and verb   in the hollow bones of a bird.
          All the way
                    down.

Because we came too late   but ate the buffalo tongue
the animal gave   and in the giving. Taste, Nate,
the presence of the other   *in* the other. Buffalo or bison?
Owl or   mouse?   Crave or eat? I cannot
     be exact. Cannot   extract. Yesterday's snake,
all bloody and cut,   begged me—I swear—*Help me, my
brother. Help*. In almost-human   tongue. It flicked
a final fierce,   mercy-mixed. As if death could
          fix.   As if my eye   alive.

Letter to Mary from the Snow of Buffalo Bones on the Laramie Plains

for Mary Crow

If the wind whingeing down from Laramie,
Mary, was our anguished joy, then starlight
    would most surely enter
    mouths of the dead.

If the sound of Jorge Teillier's trains roamed
from my ears to yours, fire ants of Namibia
    would forage for five rather than three
    minutes each excruciating desert noon.

If we reread *El Señor Presidente* together—this time
to the trembling leaves—then books about the occult centers
    in the spine would suddenly dissolve
    their *own* bindings, without opening.

If your book of poems, *Going Home, found*
a home, possums would give birth
    to a yet-unwritten
    fifth symphony of Brahms.

If mayflies hatched in December,
the thylacine—long considered extinct—
    would be found again, hiding
    inside a termite mound in Borneo.

Say the buffalo bones that greeted me in Colorado
when we met forty years ago spoke without speaking.
        Then the Laramie Plains would lift and
            fall, lift and fall, all the way to the Sargasso Sea.

If you translated Surrealist poems from Spanish
into Bengali rather than into English,
        then the death of the unsaid
        would finally say the saying whole.

If bones of the owl's tongue toughened
in our mouths, moths might struggle
        in the guttering candles
        of the throat.

If the snowstorm you drove home in that late night
forty-five years ago from Laramie was still
        snowing, then the ghost voice would be a girl-child
        stunned into the devotional pose of a slice of bread.

If the poems of Roberto Juarroz made love
with those of Olga Orozco, then fog
        at the close of *Casablanca* would return
        to the woeful pouch of our mouths.

If the aching wind was there to remind us
what it feels like *not* to hurt, rain would thieve

>   into our ears, then drift
>   into the hollow bones of birds.

If the ground gives out ghost moss that somehow
embraces our lungs, one plus one would always equal
>   zero—zero equaling seawater in lobster crates
>   raised from pond water in the coyote's throat.

If César Vallejo—belovèd César's *exuberant political
need to love*—told the willows to lie down, to mate
>   with a river, then *yes,* Dear Mary. The drying
>   in the rain-soaked leaves. But maybe *no.*

Letter to Reg from Cheyenne
for Reg Saner

Seems a lot of breath, Reg, to bleed. Seems a long time
since your *Climbing Into the Roots* helped plant me
in this place of dry land and hope-for-rain. Yes,
your "Sod Huts on the Plains near Aurora,
Colorado" still sings. The dark places.
The moon and its bruise. Bone-blur of granite. Schist
slip of a birth and death you showed in a hovel
against rain that blesses the sod and breeds *scarlet fever,
childbirth*—as you said—*in a mud box.*

What we leave, we have left. What is left
is never right. Listen. Come. Hear. I still recall.
Grieving the heat. Lightning without rain
over Cheyenne. That stinging moment singing
inside my mother's womb. The skeletal cage
I became. Through which I crawl this
scrawl of word-blur and stir. *Climbing Into the Roots,*
Reg, all the way down and back up.
Tree on a bluff, tree on a bluff, the aspens shiver,
mouth to mouth. All the long way
down. Indiana to Fort Collins. Livermore to Cheyenne.
Owl-scent to mouse. Forty-two miles not as the crow dies
but as turkey buzzards rip corpse to corpse.

Or carcass to carcass? What makes
the animal-dead? Are not the bodies of coyotes
corporeal in their bleed? Stench of crow dung just as human
as all our wrong-stung woes? We see. We need.
We climb a tree. Snuffle a root. The cattle drive

from here to everywhere at once. Cheyenne, forty-two miles
from Livermore as the crow flies. Across the buttes.
Across the Laramie Plains. Snakes, owls, badger dens
in the dust and dark that dims and just might. How full
the empty of our vast. The animal scratch of our lives.
And your words. Climbing me *up* from the root and back into.

Letter to Eric from Cripple Creek
for Eric Baus

Dear Eric, I should begin, "dear birds"—
your trademark phrase. You *are* what you fly through,
and your words have view. Even of the imprint
of the crippled cow in the rippled creek. I wish
I could recite your poems from beginning to
beginning. To hobble-sound the now. We're in Cripple Creek,
among miners' ghosts and debt. Burros no longer
roam. Donkey Derby Days is real. I met a man today
who's lost half a million in thirty years. He came
to Cripple Creek to gamble just the last three,
says he won ten thousand Thursday
with a royal flush. All pushed through the squint-eye
smoke of a Parliament. Wind in the moist
of his missing teeth. Tooth. Wind in the most
of his mouth. He likes to gopher-shoot. Somehow
believes I'm *no animal rights do-gooder.*

You're in Denver, a town *this* town made. Possibly large,
my word whirls through the tiniest of tongues.
Have I. Should we. Maybe in the. We are made
in the image of loss, which is how we gain
claim to staking us human. Which is how we talk
or quiet or calm. Which is henceforth and however
the man's cards. Face up, as if
in conversation with the heart
or spade of the Fates. Which visited
the man seventy-three years before, three days
after his birth. A flush here, a bird emerges
there. From the thicket. From the bush. From the speaking

few if any. *You don't realize just how much
energy is lost with talk,* the yogi told me.
It's well to keep a day or two of silence a week.

Bootsie's panting. I've given her some water. Lately,
I seem to drink what she cannot say but thinks about
eating. The carving and the ripping and the now.
How can she never grow tired of tenderly tearing flesh?
I've seen a lot of that here at Cripple, a town
I hear used to be dirt. Road. Just a donkey-pull away
from Anaconda and the manic of how the mountain
wide. How the mining mattered, letting blood
into a cup. Like a person's too-many-words. Stuck
at first, then opened for all the world
to bleed. A town that used to dirt.
A town I hear. A forest I speak.
A coin in the slot I refuse to gold.
Cripple Creek limps along, shiny now
with busloads of gamblers up from Manitou
and Colorado Springs. Even the gait of hunched women
with walkers gains with the lever's pull. Victor
is our way, a world of working class
just five miles from this death. Where the miners lived.
And their wives. Their kitchen-counter voice.

We've come to visit. The strike of 1894
somehow killed more than babies
made. Did all the blasting gravel allow
for touch? Did the restless sound
of their mouths? Did their ache?
Touch me, darling, where it hurts

is what we hear and can't. Please
forgive my. Excuse me for. Assonant
my mouth. I'm partial to my partially speak.
The breakage in the broken. The crippled
cow in the rippled creek. As are you,
dear friend. With your birdcage
bones and their extenuating
flight.

    We're on the corner of Bennett
and somewhere loud, shying down the talkative town.
You don't realize, don't know just how much.
Even when it only speaks in revolving sounds
of hotel doors swooshing their catch. In restless smoke
edging out the split tooth of a man with a Parliament
praising the Three Fates of good long
fortunate luck. The tentacles
of mouthy noise taking all the bets
away from where money needs to be. Like comfortable
talk that rips the wind right out the gut,
causing our lively to lag
just left of lonely and lost.
Or fire from the dynamite blast
of the throat. I would a word I should beg
from a bird. *Any* bird. Yours.
Mine. Its. A word
I softly broken. In Cripple Creek.
In Victor. In the cow-step and sprain.
In the hobble-sound of now.

Letter to John from Denver
for John Olson

The rain was said to dull the dog-dance, John.
        In Ed Dorn's *Gunslinger*, Gunslinger injects
a five-gallon barrel of LSD into a corpse, which awakens,
        becoming a "living Batch." This morning, dragonflies
alight upon my tongue, *become* my tongue, and merge
        with the hairy chests of dock workers Whitman loved.
To create beauty, you once told me, *honor and regret*
        all our internal dead. You were born. Here, John.
In this town of dying. Your mother's still here.
        When last you visited, you dragged three days of flu
up to the grave of Buffalo Bill atop Lookout Mountain.
        Funny how he never lived here. How they bid for his
body—all the way from North Platte—in death.
        Denver is not what it used to be. We could vomit it
out. We could night soil and strain. We could remember
        days of cow stench wafting down from Greeley.
How even this high, certain headaches drop away. *Into a corpse*,
        I say, *which awakens into a living batch*. But a batch
of what? Buff-colored hills, pride-flushed with elk. We drink
        cowboy coffee—grounds afloat in our cup.
The Denver Mint of aspens dragging the leaves-as-gold-
        coins cliché down a draw. I've seen a marmot
eat the sweat-stained armpit of a man's discarded red flannel
        plaid, barely avoiding a jeep. Your cat Toby had lives
well over nine. Remember the night he knocked Shakespeare
        from your shelf? King Lear married Lady Macbeth.
Who bore their son, Timon of Athens. All in a flurry
        of cat-spilled tea. Children learn to anticipate conflict
and negotiate death. By family. By friends. By LSD

    injected into their internal rain. I overheard zoo visitors
complain that the pygmy chimp was much larger and smaller
    than expected. If I had to convince a skeptic
of the existence of a rhesus reunion, I'd load my pipe
    with cat urine, strike a match, and infuse the world
cruel with sulfurous social relations. Could an x-ray of my
    lower lip reveal the denigration of Denver? Wind
inversions make a brown cloud bleak? Could my monkey self,
    my Buffalo Bill self, my heart steaming on a plate
of elk offal before me, possibly redeem—amidst all
    the unhung dead in a hanging city like Dodge?
Death is never that far east. Criminals, I say, deserve
    the kind of jail Bakunin and Kropotkin recommend.
I'll leave it to you to research the anatomy of anarchistic
    restraint. It is true, John, that your poems are she-
wolves in the form of a vague mustache. A compound
    mustard gas of aching as a poultice of nostalgia
warning against the vagueness of a sonorous etherealism.
    Put simply, you inject the Denver dead
with multiple ways of weeping. As all who return
    from the grave must do. On a hilltop. Overlooking
a city. From North Platte to Cody, Wyoming. All the plains
    of the buffalo dead, sung to us, low, by Woody
Guthrie. By Cisco Houston. A bleach of bone we never live
    or die or anywhere in-between.

Letter to Larry from Bellvue

for Lawrence R. Smith

This cemetery of Colorado pioneers, Larry. More than human bodies sunk in the ground. The body remembers, even as it stinks, permeating the Bingham Hill Cemetery silt.

Let me put it simply. André Breton died while giving birth to Robert Desnos. Hemorrhage on the sheet. Midwife dumping the pan of bloody water, shaking her head, sadly embracing his wife, Simone Kahn, in the anteroom.

Let me advise. Robert Desnos died while sweeping the stable and spotting pieces of Vallejo, entwined with undigested hay, in the palomino's droppings. *Deadly bacteria leading to heart failure,* the doctor pronounced, *brought on by erysipelas.*

César Vallejo gave birth to René Daumal, retrieving his chants from the ether, plucking his Sanskrit *OM* out of it like a radio receiver corralling waves, all the way from India to Peru, the revolt of French punk Simplests causing him to froth at the mouth.

René Daumal (poor René) never died. He left his body, only momentarily, in an ecstatic meditative state in Banaras. They sent the body of a dead sadhu, instead, back to France, tuberculous peacock sewn slantwise into his chest, a wire to the Consulate saying, *Monsieur Daumal has ceased to breathe.*

No, García Lorca was never shot. Is not lying in unmarked urine in Granada. His grave in Alfácar revealing only fossilized toenail clippings of primitive Icelandic ponies. Has never dissolved into the background of one of his poems, "Landscape of the Pissing Multitudes," say, or "Landscape with Two Graves and an Assyrian Hound."

The theory that Rimbaud became a gun smuggler from Abyssinia is false. He died a broken exporter of coffee beans, resembling, in stature, Sydney Greenstreet in the role of Signor Ferrari in *Casablanca* or Kasper Gutman in *The Maltese Falcon*.

Lord help the poets, Larry, who watch ESP TV. Lord help the people in these graves. In Bellvue. In Granada. In cremation ash raked into the Ganges. They have died or have not died or perhaps one day *will*. We are not sure. Though we *are* certain Jack Spicer is somewhere daily reading baseball box scores of Willie Mays and Willie McCovey.

Takahashi Shinkichi lived then died before dying one more time, only after collecting bottles of his own saliva for an exhibit of Japanese Dadaist paraphernalia. *Attention, please. Pay attention to the tongue-thrust spit of llamas at high altitude*, he reportedly said on the second of his many deathbeds.

George Seferis never died and is living in the honey-heavy baklava of Theodorakis.

Sinking. Sunken. Sunked. Names of the Bellvue dead, dying, died: Libbie Garland ("Our Darling Libbie" who died at seventeen years, five months, twenty-eight days); Barbara Bingham (who died at nineteen of a nosebleed weeks before she was to wed George Sterling); John E. Denne (eight months);

and the Colliers (two childhood deaths, four years apart).

And what of Aimé Césaire. He who Krakatoa. He who everything better than a monsoon? Last recorded, his black Caribbean grave, dislodged by a typhoon, had drifted thousands of miles south, invading the white embrace of the Antarctic.

How could our favorite communist, Yannis Ritsos, have ever been born on May Day, then die on such an American holiday as Veterans Day? (The symmetry of Nadja's lost left glove?) Last reported, he was still alive in the color red. In the pages of Stendhal's *The Red and the Black* flaking off into Dostoevsky's donkey ride.

Sterile? The coupling of a horse and a burro leads to what might be called *mule brain*? Sylvia Plath and Ann Sexton did indeed bear children before departing for the Riviera, disguised as two French ballerinas, while the world thought them both self-inflicted ground-rot.

Dear Larry. Dear Nadja in the body of a Shakespearean man-eating ogre. How many deaths you find in words escaping the page? In this verb and that? In Eastern Michigan University somehow drifting west of Ann Arbor?

Imagine words arriving before the mouth? The agony of the dead coming prior to the grave.

Imagine—these days—dying from a *nosebleed* just weeks before the wedding. Imagine a collection of saliva, warmed just right, propped in rows above the body laid out, all amber in its lamps. The body about to live or die. The body about to live *and* die.

What Thou Lovest Well. Letter to Hugo from Big Timber

Once more, I'm tasting the animal.
What Thou Lovest Well Remains Dead.
Actually, you said *American*, not
Dead, but America and death mostly agree.
I've been to places you tried to keep,
even as you gave yourself away.
The Afghani cameleer bags on the walls
of the only coffeehouse in a grain
and railroad town like Livingston.
Why, afterwards, were all the train cars
suddenly Bactrian in their rumbling backache
strain? I said copper. I said coal. I said
the Big Timber sheep ranch I lived
on never lost its stench of damp wool.
Even when sold and converted to cabins.
You try losing your Indiana hound-dog
roots in the snowfields of the Crazies
and see if you, too, will beg
to be shot at the wall, the glare
of the glaciers making you inane.

Wait. You did lose your Seattle roots—that house
on West Marginal Way—though searched them out
in the yeasty grain of lives fermenting
on barstools. Your fellow Montana drunks. How many
would lose a lung if they looked ahead years
beyond the painting of that bloody elk
bellowing, like you, the wood
above the bar? Any picture on the shelf
above the booze might mean hope,

even if that hope was learning how to die
just right. You felt marginal because a street
named *you*, just in the way it kept you as a child
from the world? I can't say *I'm* whole. So much
of me keeps flaking off into coydog
scat and their yoating down the draw.
My neighbor is once again practicing skeet,
and it's me that flies out, a clay pigeon,
bulls-eye wide, each time I hear the command to *pull*.

Honestly, dear man. I tasted the animal as it dropped
to its knee. My grandfather from Greece
loved bullfights because things won and lost
on TV each Saturday night, live from Mexico City
into Indiana's knotty pine. And stakes
were high, driven into the poor beast's
neck. I tasted the animal in the garter snake
I killed with a hoe. I will never forget
the tiny eggs at seven and vowing my life.
Tasted my father's downward glance
during Sunday visitation when, in 1959,
divorce meant a forehead scored by a year of ash,
as if we got glanders from the nose cavity
of a horse's infected breathing. Tasted it
in my first woman's trembling
I cried to touch, touching myself in her
joy-clenched face.

                Things age. Ache.
You urged we risk the sentimental.
I can only eat so much damp wool
before the bleating shears

me. There is life, and there is life.
I've said so little of Big Timber
I'm a brute. I see you in Red Lodge,
in Dillon, in Butte, among the copper mothers
of the world. So many sons have given
over to the mines. So many lungs,
like yours, opting out of difficult breathing
ways. I found a wounded rattler on the gravel
four weeks back and could not take the car
back over it to complete the kill.
It seemed to beg. Maybe we're all dying a little,
pleading out our red-quick tongue for the tires
to make it right? I tasted the animal
in the way I love you—Richard Hugo—
even after years our bodies never met.
Our animal selves left on a shelf to bellow
above bottles of whiskey about to break
a life. Or a shelf of books
we write and few if any ever read.
What Thou Lovest Well Remains Dead.
Whatever we love, whatever we fear,
we somehow kill and must love well.

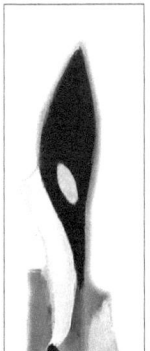

BELATING THE BUTCHERED HERD

Belating the Butchered Herd

I would momentarily remove my tongue, Crazy Horse, use it as a chisel to carve your likeness into Mount Everest.

Shall I ever be able to escape debtors' prison, I will release all ownership of sand and creek.

A horse, they tell me, is a mountain or a mount.

In South Dakota, North Dakota lies hidden, as if in the heap of a mineshaft.

They say you got off your horse during raids to position your bullets just so.

And when you did your medicine just right, you were invisible in battle.

Mourning is not a metaphor. Say our sadness just right.

We have forgotten the daring dance, the lightning of the buffalo mask, the crumbling of its tongue.

After the before-bridge across the Bering Sea, we believed all the mistaken maps with separate continents.

Shall I be lucky enough to survive, I would position myself before you to die.

All the books about you—from *The Grapes of Wrath* to *Of Wolves and Men*—are wrong.

Steinway & Sons was a German manufacturer of handmade pianos.

Gloria Stein and Gertrude Steinem were never lovers, never calmed the same dark's dark.

Words envelope words, are folded over like double zeros into a figure eight.

I would remove it. Cut it at the root, I tell you. Say thank you for all it has given me, bowing beastingly before you.

On Thanksgiving Day, the first Thanksgiving never lumbers in from the fall fields.

And the Black Hills were never smoke-tree gray.

We might rush more or less.

We might carve our mouths out into the soap of four dead presidents.

We might wash away this massacre or that, uneven the earth of Sand Creek.

Dear complete craziness of the world.

I have nothing sane to say.

I have something plain to say.

I have everything empty to play, as if a piano below the skin belated the butchered herd.

At the bottom of the ravine—at its steep—buffalo steam.

The meat tender of the brain, at its final pulse, must think, *Is this how it all actually ends?*

And still they want to fix your face into the monocle of Teddy Roosevelt.

And still they push your war whoop into Jefferson's wig.

And still they season the term "Native American" onto the quarter moon of a coin.

All the secret books about you are wrong—from *Ten Thousand Miles with a Dogsled* to *A History of Mirrors*.

Honestly, I can no longer see myself *in* myself.

Shall I ever escape who and what I do, I would fand of you my mouth, get down on all fours, and pull the load myself.

I would traces and harness and yelp.

I would find in you the broken and blurred, the black and white paint of a pinto.

I would dance the shifting shadow of my sleeve.

Pony this, grass-fed that.

Sour me something now in the sweat of the Sweet Grass Hills.

In North Dakota, South Dakota hurts.

In North Dakota, South Dakota moans, fierce and full of mending.

Fresh from the hunt, Colorado grunts up against the depths of Wyoming's Laramie Plains, sky-wide.

The letter *H* is for *husband* or *heaven* or *here-hurt-this*. When the letter *W* arrives, it knows it's only a short distance to *winter* and the letter *A*.

Even the earth sometimes gets tired of turning.

From season to season, somewhere it is spring.

Like the missing deaths of *Soap Opera Digest*, the pages pivot blank.

Your running off, for instance, with Black Buffalo Woman, making No Water jealous.

And the edited scene where John Steinbeck was to give Barry Lopez a kiss.

And Gloria and Gertrude spelling their name with a seam.

I would take it, ache my tongue back to my mouth, thank it for chiseling your cheek.

The poor pour into a steel trap, chew their paw, stagger mad from strychnine-laced meat.

To get past the censors, we bleed our ears serene, the healing scars of the mouth.

In listening to ourselves heal, the hurting hurriedly stops.

How you kept your horses fresh by walking them uphill and loping them down.

For a final ghost dance with you, dear one, I would momentarily remove my teeth.

Say your name, Crazy Horse. I would say your name backwards, three times, head turned to the left.

I would cough into the gasp, the physician's inguinal grip.

Doctor myself into a mountain or a mount.

Invisible. Invisible in battle, you could be bayoneted only in a stockade from behind.

Little Big Man, not He Dog, likely betrayed you, allowing Private Gentles (who was to die of asthma six months later) to stab you through the kidneys.

The way our animal selves paw the too-hard ground, as if the shadow of the world was real or reeling or right.

Stallions are not scallions, to be cooked with or seasoned or meat.

Here, hang me sideways. Slice me wide. Let my blood into a cup.

This horse, this crazy horse of words, would be my steed.

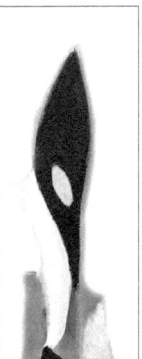

GOOD LONG ANIMAL LUCK
OF BEING ALIVE

Letter to Marie from Fort Garland
for Marie Ponsot

Your sign is the ram. You are moving
your head against anything dead.
You should open yourself
into a museum and charge a price.
We could all come through your green dark
of rainy sheep you keep on a mountain pass
in the vast lightning West, viewing tongues
you've tucked in folds we haven't broken.
You are older than me by three and a half
trees. In the way the decades ache
in two. I've always loved you
since the day before we met. The fish in my aquarium
warned me your depth. The fortune over Asian bean curd
said, *You will meet a woman soon who doesn't flinch—*
a bobcat, not a bird. We are always leaving
the protection of pines. One fort or another. Fort Garland
to Fort Lupton to Fort Here-and-Hopefully-Now.
Admit your loneliness, Marie, the impediment
of womanly strength. You are not alone. You are still
on the move. You have lived more than twice.
Your polio limp, tongue-lucked
and struck. A baby bird
winging its ache. If I looked you up,
you would certainly define
my sky. There, under *Ponsot*,
it would say, *large lightning*
on the pass between La Veta and nothing.
Tender my name as you might the road
of a glove, one finger approach

at a time. Here, touch my pulse
and let me feel ninety-eight
and you sixty-four. I want to spend
a year or two just holding your hand.

Letter to Jim from Rifle

for Jim Harrison

Jim—I want to be intimate because we've never met. Because our one letter five years ago spoke of our dogs. How mine had just left the body. All my letters are to friends. I could make an inception and reintroduce my birth. Our solitary December cries into one another. I could make myself important cooking you soup? I resist carrying firewood for Yüan Mei to his hut, prefer to live in the lantern shadow play of Stonehouse and his Zen verse. Coals, Jim. If I say enough to you we'd be seen as being warm. Friends could read by the light of the fire belching from the belly of two Sagittarians. You and I, both ruled by Jupiter, the largest planet. Both of us consuming many books. Many poems. Many lines. Lies? You eat words the crow rejects. I imagine you're at your desk right now, convulsively wanting to compose me a poem. It begins, *My dear, dearest friend.* My wife would think me important. Might let me bring that stray bluetick hound finally home. Allow me to have some woodsy thing to share with you when you visit. I might cast away vegetables and fruit, sinking for catfish regret. Bluegill and crappie. Anything we might hook—butterfly, pokeweed, poison oak—north of Traverse City.

I'm writing from Rifle because you're a good shot. Count the grouse roasting in my belly you placed there when I read your fried Swedish bread on a map. No, not Wheaton, Illinois. But Sourdough, Indiana. Spelt, South Dakota. The ancient grain in the letters of Amaranth, Alabama. I love the way you spell *James* as *Jim*. A Sagittarian poet should have a name, an animal with many syllables. Large letters. Several ways to say, *Hey, here, look at me!* Your thirty-first birthday, one day after Thomas Merton's death. That monk, yes, placed an electric cord in my throat—that's how I eat Asia. How I stumble and humble the shock of thinking my own death might never revolve beneath a Bangkok fan.

I love your work so much I'll let my lines go slack. Mary Ann says we should skip Christmas, and you and I should just buy one another December birthday things with which tender friends say hello. *Here's some chocolate, amigo Jim,* I might say, keeping me the truffle. *Good buddy,* you'd surely respond, *thanks for the whiskey you struggled back for me from a Montana bar in Livingston.* It takes a lot of meditation to carry firewood with Yüan Mei as if it were mold. We sneeze. We cough. We allow our inside cry. If I cry in your beard would you tell others we're friends of the hairiest sort? Would you say, *Imagine that, we're both born in December and we both love dogs.* That's a lot to have in common? When I woke this morning and stretched from the tie sidings of sleep, I thought I was Takahashi Shinkichi, the poet we both love. I'm not kidding. I was the monk in his poem, "Burning Oneself to Death." Parts of me singed off into what I knew was Jim Harrison soup. It was a scalding soup. Large. Sagittarian in scope. With many vegetables and much broth. Much variables and many broths. There was mulch in it from Michigan, Montana, even Arizona border seeds. All the places from which you'll one day die. *That was the best moment of the monk's life,* Takahashi begins. Like this letter, which burns on the spit with that grouse you gifted me and are roasting in my gut.

Sundog, Farmer, Warlock. Dalva, Wolf, Legends of the Fall. The human urge to procreate and blame oneself for birthing another death. To continuously feed logs to a coal-ridden womb. We're twins, Jim—father and brother, mother and son, toenail and hangnail. My wife will be impressed. I want to intimate with you because I've lost the verb "to be." Because we are or were or is. Because we met once in a letter right after my former dog left the body. You said, when she left, we have much in common. I bet you cry every December, following the Thanksgiving bird, recalling the coming anniversary of our birth. I bet you weep at the death of a cow dog. Tear-up when you realize your words give rise to me. César Vallejo placed a jail in my throat. Peruvian. Electric. Bangkok-shocked there by his translators (Merton among them). And quite dark. There is one way out and that is that there is *no* way out. When I woke this morning, I thought I was you brushing away the hairs of Yüan Mei and his load of firewood. The sound of my Indiana voice coming thin all the way from Michigan, calling me *friend, brother, ground-sniffing hound.* My wife stroked my belly, inches above my morning rise, and said she loved the stewy soup of my unwept books. My tumble and rough. My grouse-eating gruff. My legends and their fall.

(*2013*)

Snow on the Backs of Animals. Letter to Dan from Centennial
for Dan Gerber

Because there is snow on the animal's back, Dan. Snow on the backs of our tongues. Because our dogs *are* the backs of tongues. *Our* tongues. And the way we walk and pant and sleep. Whether a retriever at your side or a hound dog at mine, the Chinese poets of the T'ang held cats in their lap. Snow in the Chungnan Mountains is rain in the Sierra Nevadas. When it rains, it rains bats and frogs. The furry, reptilian parts of the heart. *Here, take this tongue,* I'd say, and you'd sense it all the way in California.

I'm in Centennial, an hour from Laramie, overlooking the Medicine Bows. We words. We timber. We wood. We shutter and mutter and splint. Wood-splints, I say, in the thick musky dusk. Remove the pituitary gland of a freshly fallen elk, and you can scent the many decades west. The road from Laramie to Centennial winds wide. And all the views of everything below are all we have lost. The heights. The dreads. Well-buckets raised from the parched throat of an owl when the night is long and starlit and minced.

I'm thinking of that fawn you wrote about, Dan, and the way coyotes cried midnight across the moon. I walked down near the Elkhorn last night, where bears den-up in the mist, and the wild-dog howls sounded my heart.

Let's say the Japanese tea ceremony included a mixture of monk hair, possum bone, and Kyoto mist. I'm serving you a cup of yourself, just in writing these words. There are at least two ways to pronounce *Sumac*, one of which sounds like the leather around our feet. What has died has died? What has died, Dan, to clothe and keep us warm? Unto what do we giveth our tongue when we say the right name through just the right slime? Snow. Snow on the backs of mammals. Their great lumbering is a Bactrian load all the way from the Gobi. There are jewels in my hand, jewels in my mouth. Spices and fires and teas. And east as west. If you misspell *mouth*, part of the word burns off into *moths* against the lamp. The way we walk and singe and sleep. Two retrievers—one on your left, one on your right. The hound dog in my heart howling all the way from Wyoming about the wrong way west. That fawn, Dan, and the way parts of us break off. Pray and die and flee. Here in Centennial, which—with rain at these heights—could be the Chungnan Mountains and the Chinese part of my heart. There, on the backs of our tongues, where we tender the names of our dogs, most loved, somehow holding what rain freezes into. Snow from the backs of all we might possibly be.

Letter to Andrew from Livingston

for Andrew Joron

Who could knock at the tender of this heart, open as a sheep
skull in buffalo grass outside the rail yards of Livingston?

Perhaps we loved a wasp and married it prematurely
with our Surrealist poems, Andrew. Perhaps we bore

a Brattleboro of bees. Of bones, you and I rejected
or denied the brittle ones of Wallace Stevens for the porous

projections of Vallejo. Green and actual avocado
was one way to soothe the silken lice of the throat.

Years of letters. We finally met in Austin, which seemed
the third and fourth paragraphs of a quite dense treaty.

I recalled blankets, whiskey, pounds of flour and sugar.
A scratchy promise to walk the woolen words of our poems

vigorously each day near a western river to incorporate habits
of muskrats and the beaver young. From Missoula,

your father's military service moved you and your family east
then west, as you searched for an extraordinary middle.

Now you breathe the bone structure of your poems, raking
rhythms in San Francisco, remembering there is a portrait

of a theremin in the Charles Russell Museum
in Great Falls that resembles a recalcitrant Appaloosa

you promised to break in time for the Livingston summer
rodeo. It was not as if we were both dead by music

or metaphor—at least not at the same time. Roof shingles
of this railroad town contain the perspiration of Calamity Jane,

when she left overseeing her whorehouse for the saloon
that night to handle the cards, discovering a man's thinning

mustache had been cheating. Back from Durango, trappers
and traders wore buckskin that resembled a wooded weeping,

strips of tree bark cringing in their fringe. Perhaps we loved
a Montana town for its rough and tumble, its hills of copper

and gold. For its railroad voice carried out of sight, east
and west at once, into the train track across from Sheep

Mountain, lantern-casting shadows and the rich mineral rinse
of the animal dead into the thick thick thickening night.

Letter to Alvaro from San Luis

for Alvaro Cardona-Hine

> "*I miss you Ramón. Ramón, we still have
> so many things to talk about.*"
> —Miguel Hernández

Compadre. We sure had fun in Truchas, reading poems,
translating Miguel Hernández, and—best—smoking Cuban
cigars—my first—beneath the pound of rain on your portico
tin roof. Our dogs later roamed your mountain yard

transforming grass into scented signs of affection.
Peemail, Mary Ann called it, which makes me wonder
what our little beagle-hound could possibly say
back to your broad-shouldered bulldogs. You say

we are brothers. Thirty years apart does not make us
a generation. One day I will die and a sparrow will emerge
from my chest. *God, it was dark in there for far too long*,
it will say. *Why did you keep a lantern all those years*

with starlight for a wick? I've come to know the way
childhurt speaks. John gave me a rag one year with kerosene
to smoke it out. Only the owl survived. Your ribcage bird
bones, Alvaro, are hollowed by Truchas wind. Terrible me.

My mouse-nest of hair hides small things like the owl's
watery wing or an afternoon shower. *Nothing's small*,
you repeat, taking me by hand back through apricot trees
to your studio. Many years ago I brought your painting

Young Sparrow home. Placed it over the piano, knowing
I somehow needed the shape of its luminous dark
green. You treat me like death. You say I am the motion
of the seventh of Jupiter's seventy-nine desolate moons.

You say with your touch, *You are a part of how and why
my life*. Surely, the Zen masters had some way to paint
the austerities of Hindu sadhus. Viyasa, they say, sat still
and meditated so long his fingernails grew into the trunk

of a nearby tree. There is nothing austere on your mountain.
We take a moment to sniff the wind. To sniff one another.
Chocho and Tula treat Bootsie like a guest, the attentive
little male, especially, flirting like an amiable older cousin.

We can learn from the logs lying in your yard
how to translate our seed. One moment we're here,
bearing fruit. The next, we're *keeping* a log, becoming
a homonym for a chronicle of our deeds. Now we've taken

the shortcut home to Livermore you and Barbara gave us.
Up through Questa and across the border into San Luis,
the oldest town in Colorado, camped at, once, by Coronado.
If I had had my way, our brother Miguel would have survived

the stiff-black-boot-in-the-face and come here to settle
his consumptive lung. Surely, he would have escaped
the Guardia Civil and become known throughout our land
as *Miguel Hernández, Father of Our Heart*. I won't say

the translation is wrong. I won't Potomac or painful
or even sorrow the snow. I know you worked all night
on the verbs. But I can tell something is missing in how our
poets mouth. Grief, they say, is a gift. Miguel would have made

San Luis right. How can a single household survive
on $14,213 a year? A child comes along, and all he can eat
is an onion. Another, and it's a boot in the face. Franco
should have stayed in his octopus ocean and drank the dark

ink himself rather than follow him here, upriver to San Luis.
Five Catholic churches, three bars, and more dogs than people.
More dogs whelped in inches, even, than annual rain. Miguel
is surely here, hiding somewhere in the sad of this town.

We're driving through and smell his enchiladas feeding
a family of five. He is calming a mother, combing her hair,
and they are eating the fascists' demise. For all I can tell,
this place is the dark green halo of paint around your young

sparrow's tail. I'm sure, now, the pain I see in your painting
The Shepherd is Miguel, a young goatherd before the Civil War,
knowing he'd be forced one day to eat the tender meat
of his own lung. The translation is correct. Our details

are younger than our thirty years apart. They misspelled
Cuesta as *Questa*, and it stuck. It stayed right there
in New Mexico across the border from wrong. Now
the misspelled Spanish *is* a ridge, sloping forever

into English's aggressive ache. San Luis remains older
than the oldest town it is. Five Catholic churches and more
bars than dogs. I know I've said the opposite. Nothing adds up
when the plight of a poet as great as Miguel goes unwept.

I already miss your cigars. The calm burn of your voice
low below melodious moments of rain. The smoke turns.
Your and Barbara's paintings still exact my stance.
The sparrow is still young enough to tell us, *You are brothers,*

you two. Compañeros del alma. Goatherds of Miguel.
Let me stay awhile longer inside you both, making the dark
green canvas-slash of so much love for one another—a simple
tongue-ticking on tin—a birth-blood bleating of rain.

Letter to Tremblay from Tie Siding

for Bill Tremblay

I'm going to call you by your last name in the title,
Bill, because you were like a kindly football coach. Someone
I hadn't known I needed, as if what you taught me
wasn't just poems but how to loosen the nails
on the siding of the house. My house. The one
with shame. 1980 seems a long life away. July.
U-Haul packed with stuff I didn't much need.
I thought I was coming a long way to Fort Collins.
In some ways not. You were younger then
than I am now—by nearly two and a half decades—
and you seemed so old. *You were born old,*
is what the father in *It's a Wonderful Life*
told his son George. And you were too. Which is likely why
you could see it in me. The boards. The doors.
The scaffolding that one day needed to be pried. Loose
in Tie Siding, I'm just eight miles across the border
into Wyoming. Cowboys still calm here
the plains. The only building in town,
a combination post office and flea
market, could be a set for a lonesome
Western script. Somebody inside
is surely tough, tearing to songs of lost
love, itching through a drunken grin
for a fist. I was never tough in that way,
but there was strength. Somehow
divorce at age three can skin a boy alive
and leave the carcass to rot. Only the farm kids
wore coveralls. There's teenage cologne.
Years of jokes. Booze, which brings its own dying

scent. Something you knew, with Crumley
that night in the parking lot of the Charco-Broiler
off Mulberry in the Fort. Your whiskey, too,
there as wind-slash for the fathers
you nor I had. I've always loved
Tie Siding because it's simple. How much
can possibly gut-punch in one sad tree lot
by one sagging ceiling off a lone Wyoming road?
How much is obscured? Seen? Cut
log upon cut log. Like lines
of a poem that can make or break.
Lines that might leave us looking pretty
without delving down into the urgency of now.
My house was rough. Untreated cedar planks
from Cedar Lake. Till Indiana teen years
brought splinters and the wet. Yours
was football stadium noise, not unlike
"The Big House" in Ann Arbor, though you came
from further east. And you tried to silence
it—even the cheers—in those days, with football
and the angels of Blake. Pioneering a town
like Fort Collins back then, wearing a hat
with the Star of Mao, made you tough up
at the bars among all the Stetsons. The body gets stiff,
holds the past. Shoulders ache. Words get stuck.
If we're not careful the poems slow, leeching off
into others like cut blood. Fathers abandon sons.
Sons hide it in siding. All the untreated
years that absorb stain. I don't much like
extended metaphors unless, of course, they elongate our lives.
Which is what our poems must do, even if the lengthening

is not time but depth. Remember our friend
Gene Hoffman? He said, *Time is wider than it is long.*
Which means only depth in this country
we claim big-sky wide. You meant that too, pushing
finally the bottle away, prodding
me into saying what needed to be dead. Now,
the tie hacks are gone since the railroad
tie industry quit many years
back. Too many trees were floated down
the Poudre from the North Fork
into a logjam in LaPorte. Things got stuck.
They needed to pry. Even dynamite
could only free so much. Okay, if we want
what poetry can grieve, metaphors too must die
to the hurt we need to speak inside.
You taught me that, although in saying so
just now my phrase goes flat.
Let me say thanks and leave it at love.

Letter to Sam from Crow Agency
for Sam Hyde

This place is rain and ache. This place is no rain but strained. History hurts. Our mission here is gas, suddenly outside the borders of the fifty States. Decades past, whiskey, blankets, and rifles were the trade. Something in the weather says Custer. In the name. Three crows circle, cawing back to the Little Bighorn and crosses Mary Ann and I just bowed to on a bluff. We bowed just as long to unmarked braves. To receive a shadow as an uninvited houseguest can undo wind gusts in the throat? Mark our mouths with unnamed stones? Fragile as fish eggs, the most civil disobedience is an act worthy of Thoreau's unpaid tax. An exchange of mutual lunacy between wars inside and out?

No, I haven't gone mad, Sam, though we're only miles from the Crazy Mountains. Montana's first dude ranch opened there in 1911. I know. Far too many details. Perhaps they hurt my poems. I get most from books I've bought from you. Other people's thoughts. Perhaps yours as they pass through your bookseller's hand. It's not what's *in* a book but the human touch it absorbs person to person. Book-must to dust.

If I said the transmigration of souls could not keep up with excretions of Bolivian honeybees, would you accuse me of plagiarism? Say I saw far ahead into Emerson's karmic past? Lingered too many evenings, after closing, in the aisle of Science and Nature? If I spoke low tones about wool ranching Sweet Grass County, near Crow Agency, could I make the world more beautiful, the bah bah bawling of a saying like *homelier'n a sheared sheep*?

Mary Ann says we all need a third place—beyond work and home. What about the circling crows? Where do they go for shade? I imagine you're in the shop now, sloshing beer after closing, a Moosehead or Dragon's Milk or even just conversation, with Dave and Gary. Julia and Mark. Or Tasha, Jay, and Johnny C. I have forty-three Jim Harrison books back home, half bought from you, so perhaps you're on my shelf too? Standing with me in Crow Agency, just outside the States, pumping gas? I often come in just to chat. As often to buy books or swap doubles. Recently, I traded a story for a book, a sad tale of the stray bluetick hound I could not give a home. *Nothing prettier than a speckled pup*, Bobby said last autumn down in Cataract Falls. He and I held beagles all afternoon, measured the slant of four o'clock sun by the length of their eight-week-old ears.

I swear I could give it all up to raise hounds, snoozing winter evenings with them before the fire, holding a book on my lap I may or may not read. Osmosis of words through the permeable skin? What do we absorb through touch? We see, you and I, things in one another we never speak. Tell me, do I *hide* at Hyde Brothers Books? Mind traplines of words? Do I uncover skins of animals, cured and tanned, on shelves of what is otherwise alive? Is my Jekyll-self waiting between this cover or that to scare me with the clout of a deranged noun?

You say I'm out of metaphors. You sound like the aching rain. Say the world cannot possibly be eaten, for if it was it would surely become turds. I'm thinking of Bolivian bees excreting honey. Thinking how too many details cloud my mouth. Say no. You're talking to four storerooms of books. Curwood,

Harrison, Doig. Goodall, Gould, Waters. The stoic posture of the Library of Heritage Press locked in the stiff upper lip of a slipcase.

Nothing stoic in the Apsáalooke stumbling toward me. Whiskey in a bag, rifle long gone. Fry bread so old it's sore. I somehow brought Custer back to Crow Agency from the dead. What passes between him and me at the pump when I buy or don't buy bread? What passes between you and me, fireside, as I sit alone with my beagle-hound each evening and read? The texture of your hand across the transom of a past before Kindle kissed the covers goodbye. What is the sound of one book closing? If a spider eats a fly, and a mouse eats the spider, and an owl eats the mouse, what part of us is killed when the hunter shoots the pheasant in a fall field late one day, its tail in full amorous bloom?

Letter to Megan from Rifle

for Megan King Hester

I promised I couldn't write away the violence
of guns, though I'd try. No one can right
what's dead, or make a thumbprint somehow
inhabit the torn bed of the left big toe.
Wolves are dogs are cats exact as hyena
scat. *That doesn't make sense*, I can already
hear you say, miles away
in Indiana. But you're the woman with bees
in your throat, calling them all the way up
from their thirty-six-year hive
and your three-year-old self into being
a still-stung woman—the age and ache you still cry.
Yes, they're there, in the throat, in the chest, welling up
through the sole of the foot like bullet holes
of poverty and dirt here in Rifle.
A town of 9,172, not counting the cats,
something you might put into a song
when you strum the chords
for "Come Down" or "The Wolves"—
though are the strings of your Gibson
really made of catgut? I dreamed that an old Chinese poet
once said, *Sometimes the dead keep on dying through our own
private bloodletting*. Our dogs may know why
they carry the mystery-rich scent
of female names like *left* and *right*, *I* and *Thou*,
here and *hair*—any dichotomous thing
simple enough to plague away the koan
of why we suffer and human and have
and hold and this day forward. There are verbs

we never dreamed. Holes complicating our words.
There are many ways to be human.
We call ourselves Luna and Bootsie and are,
for a moment, content, our animal skin thick
with the dogs that love us and with the many lives before,
the minute blood-passings we traveled
from the bottom of the now-dead world
just to become human.

                      So there is the echolalia
of cattle-gut calves, here, shuffling to their death
in a Colorado ranching town off I-70,
somehow reverberating in your Indiana
lake. So there is the buckshot of Rifle Creek,
which got its name when a nineteenth-century
trapper forgot his gun near the mouth
of the Colorado River. So there
are moments of dark and blight, this and that,
family members who said too much
too soon—and all of it lodged in the blonde
way of your hair. It lies that way, cups the shoulder,
as if it needed something to lean on.
We all need someone or something. I see
it here in Rifle, grateful that I don't
have to stay, wondering how my words might
make my mouth, might add a single chord to what
you compose. Whole armies of termites
make one tiny mound in Rifle
the entire Eastern Front where Russians died
for a Czar they didn't love. The world
goes on and on. The war, Tu Fu wept in Loyang—

as far back as the eighth-century—
does the same. Whether in Rifle or Fort Wayne
or your tiny Indiana woods
of Hoffman Lake, snow is always falling
into eventual melt. I promised
I wouldn't preach. I left my thumbprint
on your cup of gorgeous green tea. Is it
still there, Meg? Is my own private clutching
pressing the cup? Is my own shoulder-length hair
still tableside, leaning on you and yours?
There are many ways to be human.
We call ourselves Luna and Bootsie—even
Normandy and Barney, if we name the dogs
we've lost—and remember our good long animal luck
of being alive.

The Branch Will Not Break. Letter to Kevin from Livermore
for Kevin Stein

We both grew up on the other side
of the river, Kevin. You, overlooking
Nestlé and GM in Anderson. Me,
emerging from the swampy dark
of Cedar Lake woods. Indiana held us
back from parts of ourselves our tongues had
not yet known how to sing. James Wright
looking in our direction, all the way
across Ohio. He turned his gaze
from the iron factories of Wheeling,
West Virginia, on the other side
of *his* river to offer a meal of horse manure
and fish. Northern pike is not just a species
of catch and release but something as necessary
as torn shirt cuffs from childhood. Marbles
dealt in dirt. A two dollar ticket
to the movie show in Lowell. Our grinding gut
when we thought the right girl came along in high school
but who didn't see our offerings of railroad rust
and swamp ruts granting a patina of praise for the world.

I'm saying things wrong because I don't yet know
the *right* word correct. How words miss
one another and skip. How people miss
one another and slip this phrase
and that. I know that I mourn
mornings of sunlight on a bowl of oranges. I know
certain weeping when I read Wang Wei
playing his lute, alone, beneath pine boughs, waiting

by the monastery gate for a monk. Or Tu Fu's roaming
the riverbank in exile. I know
the joyful climb with Mary Ann
from Fort Collins to Livermore
with a carload of groceries, the way sunset
assures the moon will enter my throat
with its magnificent work of worms trenching
pathways for words.

I imagine your long years of loving
when you and Deb brought the ashes of your dog
up your own mountain through the wind breaks
of Breckenridge. I see you 170 miles south
in red flannel, checkered in black.
How our horizontal lives always have
depth. How black and red squares
meet somewhere on the color wheel
of flush and broke. *Time is wider than it is*
long, my friend Gene used to say. You and Deb
bowing before dirt and a wind-bent pine
to the dog that remains inside you
both.

    We somehow found the right woman,
you and I. And the right dog. *Dogs*. Our moustaches,
though gray all these years late, suggest the animal
part of our brain aching rain. Remind us that horse manure
does, indeed, *blaze up into golden stones*. That spools
of moonlight jewel our words inward into all the possible light
that Indiana, even in Colorado, gives. Sunken moons
in sunken throats from swamps sunk on other sides

of the tracks. Even mulberry trees dying
on James Wright's bank of the river.
How lucky our great good fortune
to have found tongues of the dead that speak
our past in poems that connect a fallen glove
or hickory leaf to shed skin. A termite mound
to a mountain. Pulse of a possum
to a drop of rain. Pointing us back to Indiana
woods—sassafras and elm, sycamore
and oak—through branches of slimming dark
we share with each other, Kevin, and a world
we know will never break.

Letter to Hugo from Cowdry

Okay, Dick, I'm obsessed. John told me don't
start a poem but with an image stunning
disease. I'm going for conversation.
The way you dreamed. Each Montana town,
a porridge of origin left burning
the stove. We're driving through Cowdry—Mary Ann
and Bootsie and me—as if all twelve houses
were lanterns in the thatch. Only Grizzly Liquors
and the post office have a name. There's a photo
of a hanged man in an Ogallala motel
I'd rather forget. My modification is mixed, fixed
as it is on always wanting things both ways
at once. You're alive, dear man, but dead. There
is sadness in my friend, Natalie, and it is gone.
And Muncie, Indiana, will never be dropped, doe-heavy,
during deer season. Red Cloud's War was the only one
Native Peoples ever won against the troops.
And all the sandhill cranes lay eggs that contain
not the bloody Bozeman Trail but linguistic salve that hurts.

Okay, I'm obsessed with saying things right.
Commas transparent, my modification keeps incubating
me. Making me Kalispell. Making me
Missoula. Give me liberty or give me
depth. Allow the sound of my said-wrongs
to give girth to all thinning. *Air
is air in Cowdry*, the old-timer leaned
into his own face. A morning shave
is a way to get things close. *Enough*,
I might scream, about donkeys and plows

pressuring the prairie. The plains extend beyond
Cowdry as if a dead Colorado town can no longer kill
the scent of manure long in rain.

Let me put it this way: if a honey badger
bled broken plates of moon, I'd know each weasel den
from Steamboat Springs to Laramie, the cows
of Cowdry dropping milk that won't flow. This town
is so small *Wikipedia* gives
the precise number of milking pails
or popular breaths. Sanity measured in zip codes
and whiskey. And 80434 is not the number
of bottles on the shelf but words of hurt
families of love speak in winter
desperation.

          Okay, John told me don't.
Never begin a poem I could not die.
The poem starts here, he might say. My verbs
nixed. My nouns pronounced as *this* loud
and *that*. Mountain curve and perpetual plain. Colorado
and cloudy conversation. I'm looking for you—the *Richard*
in *Hugo*. Spaces you fell. Places you tendered
and toughed into tongue. Real or imagined,
I saw the fox five times in a week.
He was crossing the road in Cowdry. She was crossing
the road out as a safe place to den. Home is where
the start is—a word in a poem, a disease
that heals. The tonguing thrush of so much
unuttered blood decomposing corpse to corpse
in the large intestine of a turkey buzzard

nailed to the hollow of a trunk. All things are possibly
driving through Cowdry, through the center
of what's gone. Absence makes the heart
grow fodder. Divine provender
to intercede. What's gone is the idea
that a word spoken just so might finally make it
right. Noun the verb. Poison the preposition.
I was crossing she was crossing it was
word-spur and blur. North Park.
Woods Landing. West Laramie. I bring Cowdry
to you to disrupt the bear-tear of words.
To say you're not alone on the drive
from this ache to that. To dispel
the loud of lonely lovely in your gut.

ZEBRA HIDE OF THE HEART

Dead Skunk

It won't leave me, that dead skunk, thirty-three miles
from Fort Collins. The serum ran out
of the medicine moon, and someone minutes ahead
struck the poor thing numb. The urgent
and incessant blatting of sheep
disturbs the tranquility of the range.
Black and white are the same, that zebra hide
of the heart. It keeps saying up is hurt. Down
is dead. Neutralize the nostrils so both breaths
are one. For a long time I loved a lie
I could not tell. We could produce impressive atavisms
by simple equations that mirror minor chords.
We could place Brahms back into the belly
of sea lice ingesting a whale. Our ribs
sour down through prairie flower and now.
I grieved the music of the poor thing's death,
even where the road bends, and surely she'd grieve mine,
though with any luck it's as far ahead as the taxidermy
of a gnat. I would just as soon pursue
the study of water cures and phrenology.
*Only Ikkyu and you would write
about a dead skunk*, John joked.
It's been a long drive from there
to here. I tried its blood-soaked side
with the finger I'd reserved for my navel,
with the purposeful picking of possum lint
from my marsupial mouth. Some animals
don't seem to sleep at all,
even when dead. The mackerel
is an example of the human nightmare

of ceaseless swimming. The parrot fish
exudes a mucous blanket to protect itself,
as do yellow perch and mullet. *Only Issa
and you, amigo, could possibly thrive
all light long inside the sad thing's death.*
Skin, they tell me, is rarely human
when glimpsed in the wild. Some part of me
longs for the marsupial pulsings
of the pouch, for a possum
night without the perfect weather
of the womb. For a long time I loved a lie
and a lie loved me. Moist imprint
from life to life, tonguing me back
time and again into the intimate vowel
in the darkness of her mouth. This dark, furry
death up the mountain and down makes me
noxious with underbelly-white. Skin,
I repeat, when found in the wild,
is rarely human. In the found
of the world.

LITTLE INFINITE POEM

Letter to Bill from Fort Collins (Just Back from Polson)

for William Stafford

"[T]he voice I hear in my poems is my mother's voice. . . .
Not T.S. Eliot."
   —William Stafford

I did it again, Bill. Finding an unanswered letter,
this one from you from the eighties. I'm just back
from Polson, Montana. The place where Hugo wrote you.

I should begin, *In our town*, like so many first stirrings
in your poems. Sometimes the leaves are falling; sometimes
they're not. Daniel Boone setting out to discover

Hutchinson, Kansas, or Cedar Lake, Indiana. And the open
spaces in-between. We come from small places, you and I,
rabbit-hutch mounds of love and dirt. Our mothers gave us

voice. You taught me to know this in the ache of rain
and possible moments of mouth. You said such beautiful
words in your letter, and—young poet that I was—I didn't

know how to respond. I waited too long to understand the way
my bones could break to milk the moon. I find love in there.
My mother's voice. The way she said the world tells me

what I should have tendered you and want to now. You were
one of the most beautiful men with whom I ever shared
eggs. The Towne House on College that 1981 September

Fort Collins fog. Every time I pass it—still—even now
that it's a Starbucks with crowds, I see you there, boothed
over-easy with toast. Me "interviewing" you, but you asking *me*

questions, acting as if my twenty-five-year-old self *knew*
something about poetry. I didn't yet know how to speak, my
mouth chocked with crisp hash browns, me wanting to sift

your wisdom as if it were the cream in the coffee we sloshed
and chatted over. So I bow to you now, Bill, ashamed
it took me so long to taste the words you somehow knew

were already there. Inside me. Though you've left
the body, I answer your letter now. All these years late. Still
ashamed, but now at my mouth stuck with toast and oats.

And the emptiness in there when I reread your unanswered
note. All I could not say but hope somehow to stir
just in finally writing you, Bill. Just in saying your name.

Little Infinite Poem, Or Letter to Bob from Everywhere at Once

for Bob Arnold

Dense? Disturbed?
Cloyingly brave? I'm walking again,
four miles on a gravel mountain
road. Midnight. 7,600 feet.

> Katya, from Boxelder, urging me
> not to fill the big cat's gut;
>
> Mary Ann, groggy from sleep, mumbling me
> to take my stick;
>
> John pasting three goose feathers into an envelope,
> mailing them postage due from the bloody mouth
> of a DeKalb fox.

Red cedar walking
stick. Hand lantern from some
catalog lighting the dark
bark of coydogs down
the ridge to flush a deer. I consider:

> Whitman's late-life circumcision thinning the
> membrane between worlds, Appleman's *blind camels of
> Isfahan* somehow Icelandic ponies somehow Long
> Island oxen pulling Conestogas all the way across the
> Badlands;

César Vallejo's "The hungry man's wheel" releasing
from his chest, suddenly, at death, rutting all the scores
of snow to a boarded Orthodox cathedral in
Leningrad;

the insomnia of Richard Hugo's lost left lung;

George Seferis's meerschaum pipe smoking *him*;

Wallace Stevens' only pair of wingtip shoes, tied to
opposite feet, pointing past one another like confused
hands of clocks, everywhere at once, on his morning
walk to work.

There it is from the top
of Sheep Mountain. Lightning on the rise
over Wellington. Down the sinks
through Waverly.

Seventeen shooting stars. So much
dying, even as the universe expands.
Lorca's "Little Infinite Poem"
getting down on all fours to eat
the grass of the cemeteries. Still
moist with starlight, I float
through the swaying
pods of stars, swimming again
in the glorious womb water
of the world.

Miguel Hernández, dead from tuberculosis in Franco's cell, though living in the bloody goldfish stain, hacked up onto the turnkey's hanky;

Yannis Ritsos and Nazim Hikmet swapping prison stories, lending salve for each of their respective hemorrhoids;

Robert Desnos alive inside André Breton's saliva after being expelled from the group. After being expelled in an almost stinging moment onto the street, preserved now past Rue de Grenelle, in the avenue known as *The Museum of All Dark Water.*

Dear Bob, prince of the short,
powerful poem. You could teach me
ways of economy and thrift.
You could teach me stop.
You could teach me quick.

You ask about the lights
of Cheyenne. Still
visible on the edge
of this cloudless ocean sky. I reply,
Dear Bob, the Milky Way.
Dear Bob, the Big Dipper. Dear Bob,
a thousand and one universes. Dear Bob,
Dear Bob. Dear Bob. Laramie,
fifty-three miles away. West Laramie,

55.8. Both glowing just
a badger's tail beyond the Rawhide Flats.

I could begin my poem here, Bob,
the only one awake deep in the night's chest.
I could, Dear Bob, trim away the more.
I could Dear-Bob-it to death,
cutting a cord of Vermont
wood and burning my excess
at the stake.

We lost a moose calf just up the road
maybe a month back. *If you see a mountain
lion, make yourself appear large. Whatever
you do, don't flee—you'll be seen as prey.*
And there are bear denning
the Elkhorn, just down the ridge.

Glorious starlight. Glorious
womb water of the world.

> Gorgeous as he was, D.H. Lawrence did not know
> when to quit, how to quiet the poem, when to calm the
> radiant wind in his throat.

Letter to Sue from Durango
for Sue Tungate

I don't recall the town's name, Sue,
though it likely had Colorado's best café
pie. Mary Ann and I stopped for coffee
only, our beagle napping in back. I knew
as soon as we pulled for Durango,
that frozen slice on a steaming 1950s aqua sign,
this would always be the pie that got away.

I'm not saying yours is not as good. Probably
better. I've quoted you snow below the melt
of the Medicine Bows as one way to praise.
But for *road* pie this was it, retreating
in the rearview as I've seen so much
of my life. I've come now
to Durango to soothe the soft spots.

I've let too much in. You have too.
That's why you do social work, wending
women and men through the low places. I can't,
for all the gunfights in Durango, remember the name
of the town with the pie. Perhaps it was *Wistful*,
there on the border of *I-Better-Not-Say*
and *How-Did-My-Child-Self-Somehow-Survive?*

When I turn the map there are no names
but Ouray, Montrose, and Pagosa Springs.
I knew even as a kid I was sinking
from everyone else's years into the quicksand
of their over-exposed heart. Borders slur

my word. I won't say
I drowned. That would be cliché. Somehow

I uttered a mouthful of mud like others
wrangle wit. In Durango, I confess,
I spent the night with a stranger.
Don't be alarmed. You've known me
nearly forty years. It meant nothing.
It was merely a way to shake the road
and momentarily forget my beard.

And Mary Ann approved. The stranger
was not a woman but was this *town*
in a calming western now, built
by railroad barons to spite Animas City,
which refused the Denver & Rio Grande. Durango
is now more than gunfight and whiskey,
homesteaders and thieves. The rail has given

way to a Narrow Gauge run, seven times
a day, to Silverton on the Highline, where men died
dynamiting a shelf from hard granite. Some lost
hands. Ears. They were blasting away
their own hard place. At night, by the fire,
tuckered from the load they'd lugged all those years
from child-strain, they surely must have loved pie,

as do I. My own lost slice
trails me the way a rain-soaked stray
from the roadside might loud into me,
Drape me a towel. Bury your face in my all-day-

rain before the wood-cozy of your stove.
In what town that hound of pie found me,
I still can't say. It wasn't Silverton. Certainly

not Fairplay. Nothing's fair when we miss the train
from our stiff-lipped youth into a painful
fruit-swelling. Had I my wits, I would have parked
my coffee and surely ordered
apple—like yours—though in a heated bowl
with cream. Mary Ann says I eat like a kid.
Perhaps I'm spooning a soggy past,

prodding the soft crust for the core.
Your husband, Gene, did that, making art with armor—
crickets, lobsters, armadillos, any careful
crustacean to guard the tender and the torn.
You miss him, I know. He left ahead in search of pie.
I wish I knew in which town, that place he now abides—
any café booth between *here* and the mysterious

there that displays the steaming hope of hot coffee
softening crust on the gentle road down.
Your pie is always right. Apple. Rhubarb.
Even Paisley Pie, with that swirl
of cream cheese. You could flour-roll Kleenex, I say,
and give it taste. I hesitate to praise.
You've got a Ph.D. A woman making

her bills. Years of social work.
And all the art of your textiles and photography.
And a man equates you with pie?

Go now. Throw one in my face for my sexist sway.
How many times have you, in your profession, thrived?
In the small of how many Colorado towns?
What fabrics have you woven from dust? Particles

of flowers surge in the bend of your lens.
How can you or I ever be said
with the poise of any single slice? Through what
possibilities do we pass, without noticing the revolving signs
of our lives? We are more than women and men,
baseball and sex, cuddling and crust.
Something got inside. Something got inside

the child and almost died. When we were young,
they must have given us lard, dusted us
well, took a fork and perfectly poked
our tender places with tiny pockmarks that said
despite the coming strain we would one day survive.
I can't remember the place, can't recall most names
in fact, but call it *Wistful,* perhaps

Regret, hollering loud before the heat
for a good flour dusting and a hard pin
to roll us thin. For the pointed prongs
of the tines. And after, for a moist towel
over the sugary bowels
to allow the fruit-cooling, as the daring
western air reminds us in each savory display

what not to eat, what never to leave behind.

Letter to Roger from Gunnison

for Roger Mitchell

The killing of Curly Bill, Roger. How the Earp brothers left
Tombstone for here in a hurry. The Spanish Influenza.

Gunnison's quarantine miraculously didn't allow a single death,
even a prairie dog or grub. BB holes in the chest of a pet moth.

Someone has surely been shooting drunkenly again
at the moon. There's an auction on eBay of an old glass

negative of bluetick hounds I've been following.
Maybe I'm lucky. Maybe I'm not. Maybe the world

that tracks us town to town will never end. The vast expanse
of pasture. Intoxicating as feeling ordinary. I swear I'm not

being facetious. Blending in is sometimes what we need.
Did you come to Marxism through archery? By respecting

the labor of your physician father? Our complex body parts
are fully awake when a child dislodges the left wing of a fly,

curious about balance? Yes, animals need to politically survive.
And Kropotkin was a prince. His father, before him, too.

The means of production, he says in *The Conquest of Bread*,
should be guided by termites, impersonating a bull ant. Okay,

it was *me* who said that. Sometimes there's death by family.
Other times, a dust-covered palomino coal-steps through

the brain. Last week, driving home from Laramie, I swear I felt
the blatting of sheep seep through the cilia of my right ear,

crawl all the way down from pastures of the Medicine Bows.
Don't forget, my thorax leaked grief over a dead dog,

that beagle-hound I held and hold and will never let go.
The ribcage around the heart jiggles from time to time,

small breaths that keep the fire swooshing. What was it like
for Wyatt Earp to rekindle a romance with Josie Marcus?

How many nights did his common-law wife, Mattie, weep?
Why did Doc Holliday leave them, moving on to Pueblo,

then Denver? I keep asking myself answers. Questioning you
as if you're me. Some paramecia can reproduce asexually.

According to the U.S. Census, Gunnison has a total
of 3.2 square miles. All of it land, none of it water.

Where do calipers go to measure the difference between
flathead and cutthroat trout? How can our amoeba selves

ever be fully seen without a microscope? How many
scissors does it take just to become human, to rip apart

our long-longing heart? I keep answering myself
with exceptions. Answering your poems. Your father

would know, convinced you, too, should have become
a doctor. Was it here, or Colorado Mountain College, where

you taught summers? I'm going to pin a moth to the dark
velvet of my mouth and imagine it here. We have been friends

forty-two years. In ant-years, we've known each other longer
than a chain of bee intestines that could reach the moon

from anywhere in Arizona. You *are* a doctor, Roger, birthing
poems, slapping them into their first wailing, examining

the sometimes-questionable breathing of friends in this line
of poetry or that. Tombstone is a name bold enough to honor

the longest and loneliest nap. Pagosa Springs, a cleansing rest,
until we realize we are all indelibly human. 1918 took the lives

of far too many gnats, delirious in the multiple rooms
of weeping. I'm thinking of 1882. Tombstone. The Earps'

intelligence to flee. To spur their ponies onward
through mountain-blur and snow, across Monarch Pass

and all its weather of a wingèd bleed. Imagine you with me
here. In Gunnison. You and me together tracking the Earps

into the blowing north. What word. What urge.
Whatever it means to flee the dust, pursue the new.

Letter to Lisa from the In-Between

for Lisa Zimmerman, in memory of your belovèd shepherd, Pharoah

It's the in-between time. What we love most
returns to the place from which the moon glows.
Parts of us are partially torn, most—
not just part—of the time. When we lose a dog
our animal bodies scream. We tear our hair.
We pound the salt. We recognize
the centuries, the many lives it took
to arrive here, bowing before a pot
of oolong. Smelling the morning glories.
Before our oats. When we lose a dog
like your belovèd Pharoah, we know more
why the ancient Egyptians made elaborate elongations
of the in-between. Why the classical Greeks
hailed the hecatombs. The Peruvian shamans,
the precise placement of maca
and salt. Those portals where nothing
makes sense. How the sperm and ovum unite,
and we come into these bodies.
And leave. I'm writing from Indiana.
I'm writing from Livermore, Colorado.
I'm writing from inside this May rain
soaking the Midwest hollers, whingeing in
from across the Laramie Plains.
There is a cure below the sycamore,
a weeping from a core of buffalo bones
from which the cottonwood sprouts.
There's a species of wind, I understand,
that will never go extinct. It blows

and blows as if trying to extinguish itself.
As if trying to give itself life. A wind
to which we return when the breath goes
out. *Please*, I pray each night, *let our animals
thrive*. Let them speak. Let the tongues
with which *we* speak. Let our blood
into a cup. Let our animals know
the portals are nothing. That the many lives.
How the sperm and ovum. How we tear
our hair. How the cure. The core.
How parts of us are torn
most all the time. The many lives
it takes. Our voices sore. The many
lives our animals breathe
into us and through.

Letter to John from Bellvue

for John Zimmerman

It's hard to begin, *Dear John*, because we remain faithful,
friend. I want to say your practice is healing, cooking,
and haiku. Of course, there's Lisa and kids. But the angel

caduceus of chiropractic replacing the twin snakes of Hermes
says Daniel David Palmer was right—that correcting vertebral
subluxation can restore a man's ear. I'm visiting the cemetery

off Bingham Hill Road in Bellvue, one of the oldest
in Larimer County, but I can't hear the dead, only low moans
of cattle up the rise. I try to remember the names. When I

turn, they float cottonwood down the Poudre. Still,
there's poor Barbara Bingham, only nineteen. Dead weeks
before wedding George Sterling. I sense the way

they should have arm-in-armed. It's Libbie Garland
that breaks my eye. *17 yrs, 5 ms, 28 ds.* chiseled into now.
Our Darling Libbie, her parents inscribed. Makes me wonder

how could they have ever survived 1890? How can you
keep healing the sore? Pouring your chiropractor hand
through dry water of the body takes skill. You might adjust

the spine and wrangle a wrist. Tug a toe through the tragus
of the ear. Calm the noxious nerves of the throat, mouthing
Libbie, Our Darling Libbie into the lower lumbar

of the first patient named Elizabeth who walks through
your door. Perhaps you should leave the office, invite her
home, cook chicken soup to soothe her back, read to her

your haiku. 5-7-5 is more alive than 17-5-28, the sum of her
years. I recall afternoons with your view. Food begetting
food. The way your loaf of bread brought olives, then

cheese. Giving up, finally, to soup. Birth has always been
tough. Torn as we are from starlight, the first days
are moist struggles with skin. There was, of course,

John E. Denne, January 24, 1873–September 13 of the same
year. And the Colliers, two childhood deaths, four years
apart. I could come apart if I lived in this seam

between sun and less sun, river and ash. I can't
count all the unmarked stones for fear my math won't
work. I have ten fingers and toes that will all one day

dust. Numbers might dessert me, the way summer surely did
these pioneers. You have read about most, have read nearly
everything, it seems, from the history of Livermore

and the Poudre, to Shelldrake, Ramakrishna, and Grof.
Somehow cracking people's backs is opening the spine
of a book, lending insight into your how and maybe and why.

We pour the kerosene, dim the lamps. Mourn the nightly
moths of what most of us miss. Mostly you read yourself,
x-ray man pouring into and through the complex organs

of the day. The cemetery tells me there are vast bodies
of stars grazing their way on cheatgrass, wild iris, and phlox.
That bodies of dust and bodies of star blur us back to word-

stir and slur, compose us, purpose our poems, made of mud
and days of sun-baked hard. We don't write. Writing writes *us*,
just as wind in the grass combs the length of our hair.

Just as people who pass pass through us, often unnoticed
in the lowing of cows. There is peace. There is less peace.
There is depth. There is Libbie and Barbara and scar. I know

you know this place, have lived just up the road in the canyon
called Rist so many people ago it shows. In our faces. Our
hands. In the gray sway of age. In the afternoon fruit

we choose. In Fort Collins. In Bellvue, here, among hay
and the languid long of the dead. Mourners stood before us
passing food over graves. Lord knows we know each other

well, our weakness and our gain. Know more than most.
I can't imagine one of us staring one day down at the other
in dread. Go get the olives—my friend—the cheese, the bread.

Letter to Jim from Boulder
for James Grabill

Your voice and my voice in the voicings of the wind.

Say we had no voice except the throat-stuck. Duncan called it, *Roots and Branches*. Vallejo, *What the tongue aged to say.* The trees call it, *All the leaves come home.*

Yes, tenses mix. Voices cross time. Which we eat all the rains and drifts of.

I'm in Boulder, Jim, where we bought books together so many pages ago now. So many deeply bit poems. Where we ate falafel and pizza and drank coffee black as the volcanic lapse of the moon.

Now you're back in Portland. Poised with your poems on the edge of a marsh moistening the mouth.

Collide. Our dream worlds often align. Sometimes in the veins of an underground cabbage. Sometimes in a John Haines poem we might read by chance at the same moment, miles apart, from *The Stone Harp*. Once, even, in one of Richard Hugo's lakes.

The mud-depths of our past crawl forth lifetimes in this thatch hut or that. In a dead porcupine pointing north. In a stand of aspen we once called *the shivering gold of the world.*

Roots and Branches, Jim. The tongue aged and saged. Your voice my voice and the windings of wind.

Letter to Gerrit from Aurora

for Gerrit Lansing

On the plains east of Denver, near Aurora, sod huts lift a pioneer past. Saying how the earth rises up to eat us. Kali Ma—you told me, the night we met, Gerrit—devours her young, transforming careful cattle-step into cosmic crust. It hurts to love this much. This deep. A weed is not the enemy. A dirty word. I repudiate the icicle of summer. I am completely Arctic, Hudson in my fur, in my response to the readings for the day—from Cixous to Bakunin to Francis Ponge. Even to *The Secret Life of Plants*. The decisiveness of a doorknob. The switchblade's flung-sung. Music of the rib, especially when the breaths cease. The silky vulnerability of female underarm hair. *The Heavenly Tree*, you wrote, *Grows Downward*. The tree of yoga, body inverted, has hair as roots. Pushes particles of groin-fire up, back into the coal-shiver of the brain. Was it Sumeria or here in Aurora where we first met? How many lives ago? Friendship like ours doesn't just speak. Which of us wrote a love note to the moon, begging it to enter, slantwise, our throat? The Lansings of Albany—our friend Don Byrd once told me—spoke beauty. The lancings of Medieval England bloodlet disease, perforating the pluckings of a lute. When Wang Wei played *his* lute, pine trees bowed before him to drink of the willow? No. Wang Wei painted his toenails with turmeric, the forest rising to coat his throat with pine wind and hermit sage. How many men knelt? How many women in sod huts died in Aurora during childbirth? How many souls rushed to incarnate—at that place, at that time, on the Colorado plains—only to leave a three-day-old infant at the great edge of an echo?

My neighbor died this morning, passing one breath into the next. Eighteen years we breathed through one another, across the driveway, through the cedar siding, as we slept not thirty feet apart. It was sad as the sudden dust of childbirth up-thrust from the plains. Suddenly, I am middle-aged. More than sixty. I almost brought home the stray bluetick hound yesterday, even though my wife refused again and again. The blue and gray mottled ticking of my life is all mixed up, showing more and more through. Something clocked in Colorado's sun-dead pines.

Last summer, the power stopped. Mary Ann and I fled a weekend to air-conditioned relief. Each night, outside the hotel so my beagle could pee, I saw a gorgeous short-skirted woman enter and leave with various men. She kept complimenting my dog. Each morning, we small-talked—my hound sniffing weeds—over her first cigarette of the day. Baggy t-shirt, bare feet, no-makeup mornings. The beautiful sore of her somewhat hoarse throat. Still, those gorgeous hips. Belle Watling. Bree Daniels. Baby Doe Tabor. I remembered all the wrong. The unsung drive keeping men alive. Killing them, one lay at a time.

There is a whalebone corset complaining my throat. *The Garland of Letters*, you told me thirty-three years ago, was the Tantric book of vowels I most need. You tell me now your heart beats weak. I hear it across the country loud as mouths, even as I hear clacking Conestogas rutting still the ruts. Here near Aurora's sad-dried sod. Huts. Buried like birth cords beneath what we can see. Quaking the ache. Deepening the Missouri Breaks.

Letter to John from Ouray
for John Tritica

All these Johns in my life. You'd think I'd sold my body
of words. Olson. Zimmerman. Haines. All three toughening
my tongue. Trebling my lip. Perhaps no poem has received

as much intelligent commentary throughout the history
of the world as "How to Die without Really Trying,"
those contiguous lines written by Everyone, added to,

collectively, at each count of three. Should the journey
reach an end, Roethke would drive that car off the gravel,
finally, clearing the ruts and grunt of the "North American

Sequence." His soundscapes, vegetal? Hothouse-clean?
He meets his leafy shadow in a place not unlike Ouray.
Even as I pass through in summer. Even as mountains

swallow the sun here at precisely 7:33. *Kagura*, as defined
by the slunk of my left gray sock, is an event performed
in rural Japan for the prolongation of life. Would it be

a mistake to read Chinese? To finally hang that deathbed
photo of Arthur Waley in my meditation room, facing east?
How might I conjure? What would the Aghoris in Banaras

advise, our bodies smeared that summer in cremation ash?
And the animals. 1875's silver and gold. Ouray had more
horses and mules than people. You're in Albuquerque,

John, holding a bundle of fire ants, reciting the poems
of Mary and Gene. Inviting me into your desert throat
of bees. Don't make me obsess. If you read the books

of James Oliver Curwood, you'd know the Far North cold
in 1912 or '13. The importance of maintaining names in threes.
Not like two-named Everson. Otherwise known as Brother

Antoninus. Otherwise known as *The-Frock-Who-Fell-
in-Love-with-the-Gorgeous-Hips-of-a-Dark-Haired-Ache.*
How many aches did Ouray have when the indigenous

tribes moved through? Whites called it after a chief of peace.
I say things in threes. Call it *Moon-Lathed-Waves.* Call it
Gorgeous-Horde-Before. Refer to it sometimes in fours

as *Sanctuary-North-of-Tritica.* Will you visit us this summer
in Livermore? Carry the ash of Mary and Gene? Cross
Red Mountain Pass, stopping in Ouray to lunch at 3:03

before pressing on, to me? Will you lug the Slavic mystery
of your middle name? The third thing, rarely seen, even when
we lose a name to grief? Will you pass through Truchas

and three-syllabled Alvaro? Bring me three hugs
from three-named Alvaro Cardona-Hine? Tritica—
remember—is precisely three beats. Mary Rising Higgins,

three names. Gene Frumkin, only two—like enormous
bookends. A cruel duel with youth. A first breath. A lapse.
Holding the tenuous tongues of retreat. You and me

in-between—a pair of compadres—knocking on wood, John. Avoiding the cracks. Washing the salt. The names of the deceased. Passing through the possibility of threes.

Letter to Tony from Cheyenne Wells
for Tony Trigilio

> *"These lines that lift their backs up in the middle—span-worm lines, we may call them—are not to be commended for common use because some great poets have now and then admitted them. They have invaded some of our recent poetry as the canker-worms gather on our elms in June. Emerson has one or two of them here and there, but they never swarm on his leaves so as to frighten us away from their neighborhood."*
> —Oliver Wendell Holmes

And so we come to a special application of death.
All this has an Old Testament tone.

Idealism denies the existence of scarlet fever in a sod hut on
    the Colorado plains, eighteen miles west of the Kansas state
    line.
Otherwise known as, *Measure this mouth*. Otherwise known as,
    One can be loved and seen that deeply.

In the next to last chapter, *A plant grows from the left big toe*.
Hidden amid underfur and long, coarse guard hairs are the
    porcupine's 30,000 barbed quills, some three inches long.

I dreamt I was writing a Zen poem to Alvaro. Economic.
    Compressed.
I kept saying *One* everything. *One this, One that. One mind.
    One breath. One soundly sleeping dog* (okay—I confess—two
    affectionate hounds).

Feel the full milk in the throat, building each twenty-eight days:
    a mountain lake due west, where forever happens all at
    once amid golden shivering aspens, talus and scree.

How do you make each boulder, Tony, seem seen? Large?
    Quiet as you are in Rogers Park? In the Chicago Loop?
    Amidst the gesso scrapings of Magritte across the street on
    the second floor of the Art Institute's south wing?

If I said a train crawled from the coals of my chest, would you
    call me the fireplace brick in Magritte's *Time Transfixed*?
If I sat hours before Delvaux's *The Village of the Mermaids*,
    would you forgive the agony of my jeans, my arm hair
    rising and falling like eelgrass in wind?

The Cheyenne had a well, here, for water. A regular stop on
    the stagecoach from Kansas City to Denver.
Miles of your meditation flow toward me. Like span-worms.
    Like canker-worms exciting the lines.

One breath. The seer and the seen. The mermaid and the ache.
One hound dog. Two. One stray bluetick, euthanized last week.
    One rescued. 30,000 loosely anchored quills. Never released.

We write whatever instrument the world gifts us. A tongue
    toughened and torn.
How, exactly, Whitman came to be published in *Harper's*
    Weekly remains beautifully unclear.

First, the visitation. The tongue of flame, in divine lovemaking,
    going down his throat, into the tender breast.
Then his desire to procreate. Long pliable lines, messy.
    Languidly lull.

Thus, it is with some ontological trepidation we might posit that Ginsberg only wore one shoe, ate with one chopstick, spoke with just one ear.
I think of your book on Buddhism and Ginsberg, Tony.
    Chapter One. Page one. Line thirty-three.

The agony and the ache. How scarlet fever got passed child to child. Sod to sod. Wichita to Dodge. Dodge City all the way to Cheyenne Wells.
What was it that passed to the mother from the daughter's limbs, suddenly limp?

The writer who draws this portrait must have similar characteristics to one of Delvaux's nudes.
Even to the women clothed against salt and wind.

One Whitman. Two. One fastidious demand of the body begging the brushstroke for more.
Too much has been made of Emerson's mysticism, it is said. *He never let go the string of his balloon. Never blew the breath of his mind entirely back into his own heart.*

One inquisitive timber wolf. Head tilted. Ear cocked. Less timber than wolf.
Otherwise known as, *Measure this mouth.* Otherwise known as, *Gorgeous mountain meadow vole excavating the body's holes.*

I hate to be gazed upon, Tony—*that* deeply.
The palpitating hearts of the night animals shiver at the scream of a rabbit carried off by an owl, all the way nearly to Kansas, sounding very much like a human child.

Letter to Hugo from Kicking Horse Reservoir

It took me forty years to arrive, Dick.
I'm standing on the banks of all you loved
and all you killed to get here. Remembering
Horsetooth Reservoir. Fort Collins, Colorado.
1980. Me reading for the first time
what was to become one of my favorite books.
I don't know what it's like to desert walk
for forty years. I know what it's been to step west.
East for you. To be twenty-four and find myself
at Horsetooth Reservoir, convinced it was
Kicking Horse, in Montana. I might sift
the gravel banks of what was somehow my
life. If I were an animal, I'd be an owl.
I'd be the night wind in its belly. I'd be
the parasite feeding midnight. Feeding
on midnight. I've broken
the thin ribs of speech like mice
bone so many times my teeth ache.

If the wind from Wilsall were my name,
the world would be calling me,
Stop Here and Listen. Finally, my mother
is a cup of oolong tea the color
of waves in this lake. You killed
a woman here and killed half yourself.
It's the age and ache of your own left lung
the doctors took and left lying in a heap.
We breathe as if we will reach forever.

I've just been to Glacier, searched the mountain goat
crags, and still don't know whether

I'm sane. Standing here, finally
at the shore of what made you
speak, I am more and less myself. Kicking the gravel
loose as you have, I see parts of myself
are chipped smoke and dust. This land is Salish.
This land is rain and when-will-it-come. This place
is a tongue I came to loosen and say moments
I could not speak. Something is always uttering me
in the gut, at Horsetooth, from forty years back.
Especially now at Kicking Horse. It is September
but not as late as August when the moon pours kerosene
down my stillborn throat. I am ancient
in my skin. I have slept too long and not
long enough. I have eaten the animal.
The animal has eaten me. Its tongue,
decades deprived, toughened and torn.
I *pray hard to weather*—
what you called *that lone surviving god*.
It took me forty years to arrive.

ALL THE PATIENCE OF BROTH

Dejected in Boulder, I Think of James Wright's "Depressed by a Book of Bad Poetry, I Walk Toward an Unused Pasture and Invite the Insects to Join Me"

for John Bradley

That dream again where Yüan Mei and I
are brothers, gathering firewood
every day. Brewing roots and tea.
A kiang outside our hut most evenings,
just beyond our sleep, all the way
from Tibet.

That dream where John and I are at AWP,
but I won't leave the hotel room, nursing instead
sick birds with scraps of my poems I tear and tender
with all the patience of broth
into their weak, delicate beaks.

I've just come from Red Letter Books in Boulder,
an hour with Bootsie in the poetry stacks.
So much that is *not* Vallejo.
Language for the such of so and sake.
Every phrase seems confused. Everyone
seems to have something to say
about nothing, as if reading books
about the world, among poets, has been banned.

Then a more satisfying hour
in History, in Natural Sciences.
Astronomy. The celestial bodies
of ospreys and hawks in the insect-thick
animal night. Two of Jupiter's

seventy-nine gaseous moons hidden
in the humps of a Bactrian camel.
Marsupials with the primitive impulse
of the pouch somehow holding me
closer to rhythmic breathing than clever
language ever could.

How many evenings I've spent with Yüan Mei
before the fire, talking of woodcutting, the winter art
of mending a sock, the proper seasoning
for congee. For stewed pork. Steam rising.
Wuyi Mountain tea. He pours
himself through me as if filling a cup.
As if parting my lips would help me
follow the migration of butterflies
to a cave in Bolivia, or trouble
the black branches of the north.

The southern Tibetan Steppes. Hundreds
of miles through fog. The prance of primeval play
among ungulates. Only a few herds left of the kiang—
the ancient, wild ass. Black stripe down the center
of the back. The before world, the after.

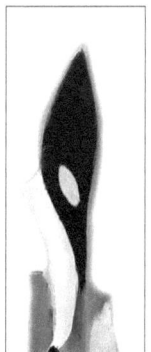

THE BRAHMS-BITTEN. THE SWEET

Letter to Forrest from Laramie

for Forrest Gander

You have the handsomest name, Forrest, east
of the Mississippi. Whole land tracts bow to you.
Fireflies fierce upon your tree. If you were here,
I'd call you *Medicine Bow Mike*. I'm sure
I'd see snowcaps increasing years in your hair,
as you'd ease down from the high-country
beaver pools for a week of whiskey and cards.
They've certainly camped in mine, refusing to leave.
Such squatters throwing snow seem to like me
more each year. In Laramie, I'm passing
through, up for the day from Colorado,
pretending I'm not already passing fast this life.
We lunched at Coal Creek, an outdoor café
that likes Bootsie, and she, the scent of cowboys
and cream. There was a Great Pyrenees named George.
He was a benevolent king. I never felt so small with him
ponying over our little hound. I thought of your deliberate
and slow. The way you make the world seem seen.
Large. Across the street, Night Heron Books is not
a woodlands goose but a hole claiming Laramie sane.
It says there's feed, and not just a bag of oats
as a horse's sling. In the store. On the shelf.
You were there, your *Deeds of Utmost
Kindness*. Which is all you say and do. *Hey Mike,*
I'd whisper if you were standing with me, leaning
into your buckskin rough. *Read me one of them fallen
sounds alone in a forest only philosophers can hear.
Gentle me, gentle man, over the timber beaver
can't wait to sink.* And you'd roll your sleeve,

drop your calm animal cap, let your blood
right there into a cup, and say that was your poem.
Then slit your best wrist all the way, saving the other
for straws. I could draw the shortest
vein and win the night watch, high on the rise,
overlooking the trains. They couple, out back,
off South First, near Big Hollow Food Co-op.
Who, such days, would name a grocery *hollow*?
Who would claim such emptiness large?
How often our want. How deep and wide
and sky. How we crawl and scrawl
and mound of emptiness, a badger
den of depth. That's where I reside, you know.
In the midnight fierce, pounding out
from the coyotes. With Lorca's ants
that can't be seen but frequent
your wrist. Mary Ann has enough sense
to draw me up from the well-depths
of dirt on the Rawhide Flats, point me
back to the marsh, which seems to be this Night Heron
Books where I find you utmost forever kind, though shelved
in the F's as if your last name was wide and dark
and reach. Imagine a bird balancing a leg, unseen
by clay, sinking into the blathering
musk of a night scent so deep we have to sing.

Letter to the Mikautadze Dance Troupe from Livermore

for Elizabeth & David Mikautadze, and for Ann Brake, Emily Craig, Kynzie Egolf, Zach Fensler, Freddy Fuelling, Kelsey Patnoude, and Ren Rivera—with gratitude for our collaboration

I don't know. Sometimes, I don't know how. You wend
like wind. You hinge. You vowel and swift through me.
You open-arm and accept my step. Receive clumsy
me. I am honored among you and through.
To walk. In the midst of. Your dance.
With my poems. Aware of my gray
and weight. Elizabeth says I'm a pine tree.
Rooted. Sixty-four years in the soil's wind
among a grove of graceful willows.

Sometimes, I don't know how to say, *Which way
to the golden yellow dead?* Or, *How can I count
the wept wings of birds?* Or, even, *Is it true
we slept the animal? Did we ever truly sleep?*

Which of us carries the birthmark of Brahms?
Which, the cruel salt flats of Coltrane or Monk?
How many sunflowers lie hidden
in the tilt of a dancer's wrist?
Whose heart did they replace secretly
one night—while we slept—with the silk
strings of a Chinese lute?

So I'm just back from Laramie. And the time
of day is now. Midnight could be noon,
if the moon was finally to be believed. And it
should be, washing—as it does—the entire valley

all the way down to the Elkhorn. My 2 a.m. cup
of oolong could be your afternoon nap,
or an ancient T'ang river in your veins
all the way from the eighth-century Wuyi Mountains.

You open and clothe. You unfurl
and fold. You anguish and ache. A peacock tail
fanning my sleep. Iridescent. Primordial
steps crawling to me. Calling forth the hound song
and shagbark hickory of my poems. And, in response,
my words bow back to you.

One of you is a bamboo parasol
propped against a temple wall in Kyoto.
One of you a swan. One, a troubadour
from Soviet Georgia plucking a panduri, with Mallarmé
on your lips. One of you is a whooping crane
practicing invisibility in a forest preserve
in Illinois. One, a seated Buddha, a golden
mountain lion not yet dead. One, a Viking shield-maiden
dreaming of Valhalla. One, a red-crowned crane
stalking the canebrake along streambed bottoms. One
of you, the offspring of a river and a willow
who might one day be buried in a Macedonian grave
among flowers and fruit. Basil, frankincense, and birch.

You keep dancing 1183 miles away
in Fort Wayne as if you, too, slept
the animal in the thin
7,600-foot air. Through thick pine branches

and pods of Colorado stars, as if floating
with me, nightly, in womb water.

You or me or the birth-bag in-between—weeping inside,
as if truly alive. As if coming once again
into these bodies, we might heal this time
and finally get it right. Like an elongated
vowel. A herd of words boiled down
to sound. A bowl of oatmeal, say—
on the table before us—creased
with chia seeds and one mashed sweet potato.

I promise to return. To you. I will poetry
and its source. I will the missing and the skipped.
I will buffalo grass and bend, touch the arch
of your instep. With my words. Grounded
in your hollow bird bones and wing, your willow-sway
stance. Come humbly, that is, carrying a postmark
and an egg. The offspring of an emu and an owl.

My words will be your dance. Your dance,
the way I inward. Move. Which of us carries
the birthmark of Brahms? Which, the sad salt
in the minor keys of Mingus and Monk? Which
wing beat will make the weeping
cease? The journey inward, the place where—
sacred, tender, trusting—we most humanly meet.

Letter to Noah from Castle Rock

for Noah Eli Gordon

Nikolai Gogol's overcoat.   A prayer for protection, Noah.
Mantric words to be   well.   How Ivan Ivanovich
quarreled with Ivan Nikiforovich. I must confess. I   do
not   understand something outrageous as   refreshed insults
at the town post. A bee   impersonating a wasp. A wasp
impersonating the placidity of a luna moth—just to be part
of Robin Blaser's   *The Moth Poem.*

You have never lied to me   except on occasion. In your
poems. That time you and Sara   fed me
gingersnaps during my   reading   at your
Denver home—just to keep me   from reciting
that poem   with the seventeen urine stains
to the onlookers   in your living room.

It is written   inside the body of each earthworm   that
an edaphic urge epitomizes great   large   luck. There are
egg-eating snakes that have not extended very far   into the
world from the whip-snap of their   original reptile brain.
Castle Rock is named   for a butte south of you by
twenty-five to thirty miles? If   I asked you to bring me
a hypodermic needle   of Mao Feng tea, would you leave
your toothpick   sculpture for an afternoon?
Rush down here with a liquid fix? Would you   say
my name while changing   your newborn, reciting away
the night soil   of the world?

What is the consciousness of a place named for fortification?
Mined   for rhyolite? Do its children grow lungs
partially   closed? Their parents' arms crossed,

say, when someone asks the weight   of the marital bed?
I have released so much   ectoplasm
                  into the carpet-   moths
here   at the Best Western   that I no longer trust rain
weather of sheep ranches   and wool.

I see you have birthed a daughter,   Georgia, who resembles
my name. Confused   the brushing of teeth
with smallpox passed blanket to   blanket. Confused
measles, mumps, and   metonymy with the malaria
of a malevolent discharge   of black water.   With
the generosity   of snakes in Castle Rock. They rattle but
never strike. Bake on the banks   of the South Platte,
sending 3 p.m. thought-waves like heat held   in stones
three hours north in   Livermore. Day.   Night. *Let him
pass*, the snakes implore their brethren. *Let his family pass.
Any time of day or night.   Grant his dogs safe journey—
                  unharmed—
without quarrel, with or   without overcoat, bees, or
                                        invocations.*

We have never lied, Noah, especially   in our poems.
Measles, mumps, metonymy. Insults   at the town   post.
A luna moth   impersonating the   cool   lunar
night. This poem,   a prayer for protection.   A safe-
haven. A well. For *my* dogs   and yours. Mantric bees
surrounding us with healthy seed-   sound   ground.
The overcoat   of Nikolai Gogol.

Letter to Jay from Boulder
for Jay Griswold

Strange how the body felt in childhood. Clumsy. Abrupt.
Shining a flashlight into the palm of my hand, fascinated
with the glow of my own young blood. Homeric shaman
journeys among the Shades. Anglo-Saxon war rhythms

merging with the Chinese *Book of Songs*. Excuse me,
but an oedipal interpretation of Emerson neglects
the transmigration of human souls from India into the body
of a Boulder osprey. In other words, Jay, I am in Boulder

among Tarot readers and transients. Followers of the great
golden crow. In other words, the world is almost round,
even when square. Even when lost among clasts
of the Flatirons. You lived here once, though spent most years

in Littleton. I recall coffee at the Trident on West Pearl.
Your four o'clock beard, as if you'd just woken at three
from a turbulent night of Vallejo. If I asked you the weather,
you're sure to say Ritsos's blind mother squatted over a beer

bottle on the island of Samos. If I asked after your health,
you'd say she buried the birth-bag inside the bodies of mites.
It is all an experiment, this thing called living. Pigeons fend
down through us. Satisfactory light for plant growth may be

replicated in a lab, if at least close enough to a source.
Possums, hardy and large, are normally kept in a cage
outdoors. Mary Ann and I come to Boulder for pizza.
For healing and books. To remember what it was like before

I gave my life to raising hounds and working to finally grasp
the almost-glimpsed in Stevens. Sun seeps down
through hens' teeth here. Through us. Our throats
incline the wealthy slide of copper gutters refusing thieves.

Before we met, Jay, I knew you inside the color green. A wolf
tooth, worked loose, corroding inside the carcass of an elk.
I saw you once in the posture of pines about to accept Boulder
County rain. I saw you in the letter *A* in every index

ever booked: Vicente Aleixandre, Antonin Artaud,
the Alkali Flats all Wyoming-wide. The best thing published
in the last ten years, I swear, is a memoir by a horse fly
that spent eighteen months inside the left nostril of a Mustang.

Poor horse could barely gather breath. The fly droned on
and on about *a tiny thermal trembling* and *a vague inside
light*. It still hurts to examine the palm of my hand. The way
blood flows from here to there. The scraping back and forth

of complex births. Shaman journeys among the Shades,
Jay. Your four o'clock shadow. A plaza in Old Town
Albuquerque crawling forth the owls. Afternoon bells
at a Kansas hanging. Juárez, Mexico, and its endless trains.

Their stutter-shove throughout the night, complaining
the track. It all seems so simple. This moving from here
to there. Even successful culturing in a lab depends upon
the tiny tremblings of leeches being released.

Letter to Phil from Red Feather Lakes
for Phil Woods

If we could just see ourselves in the eyes
of skinned-alive, Phil. If the Denver flood
that took your basement hadn't brought Rexroth
and McGrath, your Cisco Houston and Woody Guthrie,
into mold. If Red Feather Lakes hadn't been founded
on farming fox. I have two left ears. They're both
pricked for wind. Listening for Dmitri Belyaev.
For Lyudmila Trut. The rustle of their cramped cages
in Novosibirsk. How can fear and frightened
ever sigh? Science, sure, is sometimes
exact. But Red Feather fur for the sake of fashion?
All these years of meditation and I still can't forgive? I try
my heart. I try my morning toast and oats. Try bloodletting
my mood into a cup. My morning shave. So many hairs
bend like wind-ruffed fur. We read our heroes
hopping train cars in the thirties. We say *Rexroth*
and *McGrath* as if radical winds might press on.
They're busting the unions in Wisconsin,
Phil. Busting broncos, still, in Casper. In Stillwater.
In the anywhere in-between broken speech.

I heard a woman on food stamps just yesterday
lament the price of diapers. Pregnant, with two others
at her knee. All we eat turns to shit, soiling our young.
How do I sleep each night just fifteen miles south
of where they farmed fur? Upon my heart,
I promise never to drive again to Red Feather
without a prayer for the animal dead. Foxes brought

wealth. Foxes brought blood that made the acres ache.
The resort stocked trout into man-made depth.
They're frantic to get out, flopping in the rivers
of my mouth. There's a flood here in the high country.
A flood two hours south in your Denver basement. Mold
on the shelves. Mold on the soaked pages
of Rexroth and McGrath. Open their hearts
anywhere, and you will see how they continue
to care for the about-to-die. For train-hoppers, thinly
blanketed, lamenting the Pueblo dead. Open
to page thirty-eight or ten or even fifty-nine,
and hear them cry out in child-rhyme,
Red rover, red rover, let fox blood come over. God,
if I could just say it right. If I could hobo-song
and hopeful-dead and heal. If we could just see ourselves
in locomotive lanterns from the thirties that continue
tunneling past mountain scree in Colorado and Montana.
Through dust devouring Kansas. Oklahoma. Swaying
to the songs of Cisco and Woody. To the pleadings
of Rexroth and McGrath. Just see ourselves
one moment in the eyes of skinned-alive.

Letter to Michelle from Victor

for Michelle Comstock

Scrabblings of dusk. Conjugated grief. Some dead,
        dying, died. Workers working still the mines. Michelle,
                we might secondsay the heat, admit July,

Colorado-dry, into our bones. Profess to know the many
        sways. Feldspar and gold. We might bow
                before the ciborium of sunset cutting back

across this lack or that, high here in Victor.
        9,695 feet. The Colorado Labor Wars.
                Union strikes still struck. Like a lantern

about to tip. Deaths still dead. Sea-gone groan.
        The strange mouthings of primitive fish
                high in rock and tight. The way religion

promulgates the past. There was a little girl
        in a long denim skirt went door to door
                for Christ. Her father, a pastor. Her mother

saw the end of the world, all the way from Bedford,
        Indiana, to Oskaloosa. Iowa is more than farming
                animals and calm. Sometimes our past

unscrews our shoes. You step this way, that.
        Have taken strides away from Bible Belt life.
                One buckle. Two. How were you and I born

into the same breath? Why this incarnation
     here, now? Mary Ann says Victor is more
          than ghosts. The Ashanti Mining Company

stoking Rocky Mountain gold all the way back
     to Johannesburg, lugging it out of the bones
          of the many-soaked. Miners coughing dust

as if two packs of Luckies a day. Backwards,
     the lines try to survive. Slavs in Pueblo. Ludlow
          Greeks. The German dead of Victor. Dead,

dying, decried. Masked. As if. As if morality
     was not a play. Right and wrong never
          performed. As if Euripides was not a Greek.

Had never been an Athenian. *He saw the veins of men*
     as a net the gods made to catch us in like wild beasts,
          Seferis wrote. And was right. Here, now.

Just five miles southeast of Cripple Creek,
     this town can't walk. Five miles from where
          it gave the gold and built a name. Gave

all its blood and hurt. This place of graves.
     M.M. Demeree. Ella Porter. Minnie Denson.
          Two dogs named Shep. Donkey dust of mules

gone quick over the sluicey ledge. The horse
     part of the mule all panic-ear and twitch.
          We have been made by truly two, multiples

of moaning dust. We have been children far too long.
        You still walk door to door inside your ache.
                Test this latch and that. Lug the donkey dust

of your father's church into what you do
        and don't. I, too, flinch at the voice
                of strain. Parents who no longer loved,

even themselves. Who in feeling unloved
        just tried to survive. Strange mouthings of almost-
                human pain. Dry and tight in the shy animal

spine. This raccoon or that. Fox blood
        in our sleep. Possum our mouths out
                with toads. Mary Ann calls it quaint.

The old Victor Hotel. This ghost-town most. A town
        of 445. Only a brothel-turned-breakfast-joint.
                One rail of men who exhaust the mine,

hunched at the bar called The Young Buck.
        And all those boarded doors. Newspapered
                glass. Ranch-hand sad. 10,000 feet, you'd think,

would be closer to the Lord of Hosts.
        Like a lantern that in losing its grip tips heaven
                light to hay. We are all burning up inside

for mine-dusting the light? Your father
        was a church. Does well, you say,
                with grief. My mother and father

and me cleaved at age three. One one-thousand, two.
    Children's games are voice. Count the seconds
        about to be our lives. Why this life for us

this life now? You and I destined to meet?
    Victor doesn't stand for Victory but for the man
        who tossed his name into a hat. We should all

be so lucky to be christened by chance.
    Backwards, we turn to our past for shoes.
        Step inside. This foot, that. Walk with

our maculate hands. Drag our monkey-knuckled
    self to the mineral shelf. The Western Federation
        of Miners is dead as a thrown-bolt latch. Strike,

struck, strucked. Conjugate the match.
    Friction the boot. Drag the sulfur
        up through the sole of the foot

into our most-fretful stance. Secondsay
    the heat. We are here, Michelle—ingots
        of ignoble birth, brilliants of light

then dead. The strange mouthings
    of fish. Mimes caught in the pant. Fossilized
        and fixed. The sea-gone groan. Found in this

town. Found only in rock in the search for
    gold. Dynamite-blast and pick-axe stance.
        The strange strained wraithings of now.

Letter to Paul from Timnath

for Paul B. Roth

I'm in Timnath, Paul, just southeast of Fort Collins. Population 223. Former route of the Greeley, Salt Lake, and Pacific Railway. There's a graveyard. The First Presbyterian Church. An elementary school. That's about it. Oh, and the Independent Order of Odd Fellows—site of bake sales twice each year. For Reznikoff and Oppen, the ongoing concern was language in relation to objective details of the worlds we complete. The digestive tract of a dust mite resembling ours, for example. Oleander—eaten by bees—and excreted back into poisonous leaves. You know I do not exaggerate. When we lost our Colorado home that year in the wildfire, I was sure there had been an incantation I neglected to chant the year before over bodies of sunburned ants.

I understand the queen termite's abdomen continues to grow throughout her life. Eventually, she may lay as many as 34,000 eggs a day. The body of the poet has an exoskeleton of words and phrase, endings and embrace. Complex breathing cues resembling rhythmic contractions of the brain. Some hurt. Some urge. Some release a sticky substance from a cavity whose origins are lost in antiquity.

Tell me, my brother. What *is* "Marxist amnesia"? In what ways did Trotsky resemble a horse? Bolshevism was corrupted by a linguistic schism? Schism, best defined, is the burial place of Richard Hugo's diseased left lung? The one removed twenty-one months before his death? The one pulsing still in a mound of Missoula muck?

Timnath, as a town name, is severe. Weighty promise of a psalm. The fourteenth chapter of The Book of Judges. The practice of whip-slash and asp. Stones in the mouths of the banished. The place Samson found a Philistine wife. You named your magazine *The Bitter Oleander*. Words that plant. Plants that heal yet hurt. Poems that spread an umbrella across sun-slant of the untimely bled. What part of the human vowel is poison? Is the leg spur of a platypus—one of only three egg-laying mammals in the world—composed of such tender complexity, even with its venomous gall from a crural gland?

Dear Paul B. Roth. I *just* realized why you so love our dogs. Your old fella, Bodhi. My two girl-hounds, Barney and Bootsie. As long as I've known you, I never unraveled the riddle of the first letter of your middle name. Here, help me breathe. Bee intestine. Blake. Buffalo Bill. Borges. Paul Blackburn. Hugo Ball. Nanni Balestrini.

If Georges Braque were alive in Timnath, he'd also slant edgewise through your name. He'd paint a portrait of a beehive from the inside. The geometric space of workers working the work of the secret name. He'd interrogate a bee intestine, exposing slow moments of partially digested grief. He'd be an Odd Fellow, I'm sure. Build a tavern overlooking the graves—a shot-and-beer-joint shading yards of the Timnath dead—and name it *Bitter Toe Meander*. Hang a sign, out front—for all who pass—of a left foot walking away.

Letter to Kent from Fort Wayne

for Kent Johnson

Cows' breath, she said, from the wisdom of her
farm, *is one of the pleasant smells
of a barn.* So, too, the golden stones
James Wright described, as he praised the droppings
of horses. Even the bird dream
Alberti had, unknowingly, the night Cernuda
left the body. You've left Freeport and all that
scent behind. Are there hound dogs in Spokane?
Will they help you flush the comet tail
Aleixandre left lumped in your throat? The onion
Miguel Hernández wept over, imagining his infant
son with only sadness to eat? Who will soothe the burning
eye, savor the thin skin of *this* breath
and *that*, when quail boil out of the thickets,
questing for air?

I've left the West for the winter, Kent, back now
among shagbark hickory and elm, sycamore
and sassafras hollows. Oak. I'm back in Indiana,
standing in a dry creek bottom, begging the moon
to split open and let its blood into a cup.
Sure, the Milky Way is one way out.
One way into and through. The T'ang Dynasty
poets are another, the great ones
you and I somehow read the same years, together,
all those miles apart. How could we have known
we'd one day meet at the corner of Wang Wei
and Vallejo? I've said it before, too many times

to survive: we come into this body again
and again, meeting those we most need.
Sometimes those we most bleed. I've met
you two times only, maybe three. But know you
in ways the wind-swept don't. There is tenderness
in stars exploding, fierce, from too much
heat. And how our bodies are made
remains the mystery of the green peppers. Cut open,
exposed, their tiny seeds on the board glisten
as if Rubén Darío, blindfolded,
stood against the wall with a final cigarette,
relinquishing sunspots of his beard. And a cottonwood
calmed the moon to form our blood.

Please forgive me. I know. Sometimes I say
and sway and pray too much. Repeating myself
as wind, then more wind. Then more. Folded into whirls
of cows' breath and dung. One good thing, in Indiana
I can *hear* the cows breathing *you* breathing *me*.
All these snowfields apart. Poetry is like that.
We stay up till dawn, tending the moon, sloshing tea,
sailing down the Milo with Tu Fu.
Not just in mind. Not just in willow
branch and sway. But as red-crowned cranes
in the hollow-boned bodies of the dead. We tatter.
We exile. We sore-feet and cloak. We partial
in the parting snows. Words come wrong
though right into our mouths. To thrive.
We float with them, a chicken hawk
circling how and what to say. Partial

in the parting snows. Part way home.

It could be Fort Wayne, or Spokane,
or Pine Island, Minnesota. Even the damp
guard hairs of the hounds bursting through
brambles or the snowmelt swale to remind us
to keep our ear to the ground,
where poems rise through ancestry
and pain. We test our mouths. Milk our blood.
We struggle-clutch the way. Words come
and fall apart like raisins steamed loose
from the doughy dents of bread. Tell me, Kent,
how is a human life even possible?
Imagine the moment of conception, the stinging
bleed. Our insides milk-loose
from starlight into another's sorrow.
Think, again, to our first tears. How each time
we arrive weeping, as if already knowing
how difficult it will all be
to try to get it right. There,
in the wanderings of Meng Chiao,
in Tu Fu's torn, it could be us again in moldering snow
amidst the barbarian encampments
of the north.

       I want to thank you
for entering the world this time
the same decade as I did. We stir together—partial
in the partially worn—the night soil
we know must certainly be banished
to this plant or that, to Whitman's beard,

along with the grit and grief of his belovèd bees.
As we bow to the sorrow in the sorrow-mouth.
As we praise the poems we say and do.
As we circle home with the chicken hawk.
Search the fields for golden stones, smell the animal
smells of the barn we were born into and through.

Saidshaft. Letter to Mary from Albuquerque

for Mary Rising Higgins, 1944–2007

Fearless was how I described your work, the only word I could.
The way the secret and the lice, the Brahms-bitten, the release.
Fearless how the *you* became a *we*. Your *the,* an irreplaceable *a.*

So we ate *chiles rellenos* that afternoon in July and remembered
how common our seed. We talked poetry, of course, breath,
even the delicacy of my beagle's feet. So, we came to that

place where knowing knows all it possibly cannot. We ate
with you barely eating, with Paul Celan somehow there
among us in airtight tie, coaxing you down into some

unknown strain. If the sliding glass door out your backyard
were only Albuquerque. If in opening it to let out the dog,
we found ourselves slipping back in, further from what we

could never and not. Dear Mary, there are many things,
so many wants to say—sweet things, *human* things.
I want to say *hibbux,* and *hydrax,* and *root of the hyssop,*

and *saidshaft,* and *shift,* and *Here, take this tongue.*
I want to tell you, *Sleep the slept of our dearest and most deep.*
I want to say, *Here, eat the monkfish whole, but broil it first*

over the luminous rib of an owl. I wish I. I sincerely grow
a word. *Here, take this chest,* I'd say, and I'd get down
on all fours and tear the carpet apart for the pineal gland

I'd left of dust. If the sliding and the door. If the sharing
of breath over a green pepper. If the right way wrong,
the endearment, the act of loving away. If a *sopaipilla*

and honey. If that can of Coke you and Mary Ann and I shared
to give us the caffeine need we felt we'd otherwise grieve.
Hearing your poems from your bed as one final release.

Breath. Stop. Breathe. If your syntax and its kept
and its swirl as it must and *has* to and most certainly will.
All right, an airtight word is held lovingly in the throat.

This much is clear: Celan-sting of the not-quite say-so,
not-quite bee. So, we've come to that place where the air inside
a jar is the breath of the deep. Unceasing blessings, dear one.

We are all inside something twisted shut, until we find
the *sopaipilla*, the Brahms-bitten, the sweet.

(August 27, 2007)

I'm Writing Gene a Letter
for Gene Frumkin, 1928–2007

I'm writing Gene a letter, but he's dead.
I keep trying to say it's 99
in Fort Collins today but only 93
in Albuquerque. I keep trying his side
with my hand, the resurrection of his word.
Remember the Navajo man who sold us cedar?
I had a headache three days and could kill it
only in Livermore after dumping
the bundle from my backseat.

Remember the fragrance of the full moon
over Dodge? I'm writing Bob my mouth,
the tender of it and clutch. The way this word
or that. The moist imprint of my strain.
Trains don't always reach west, I'd say,
and he'd nod that rain-in-the-barrel nod
he'd use as table water in Vermont, Susan
each evening at the stitch, dirty shirt
left out on the truck to wash and dry.

I can't write Alvaro because I love him.
No one can write another they see
as themselves. No one agrees. Nothing.
Not even the pronouns. So I'm writing
Alvaro through Gene because Bob
just published his book. Alvaro's book,
not Gene's. Made by Bob's hand.
My book in a way. And Tom McGrath's,
because he kept writing Gene
a note. I keep writing

John because he's not dead, because he writes me
back each day as if I'm answering myself,
as if he's unleashed the fire ants
of Namibia again in my wrist.
In a way I'm writing Bob, though sometimes I call
him Patrick. I begin, *Dear Rain in My Chest*,
or *Dear Zhivago Platting the Full Yuriatan Moon
Over Dodge*, or *Sad, Sad Glance of the Owl*.
I call Patrick a name. *My* name. Paul's.
Barney. Bootsie. Adorable-Beagle-Breath.
Because Gene loved them both,
though he died before Bootsie arrived.

I can't write Gene because he's alive.
Somewhere busy. Marking my strain.
He keeps saying, *Hey, amigo, don't write me
anymore. I'm fried. Write Bob*, though they never met.
I think Gene wants to write Alvaro
so is asking me to write Bob.
I think John wants to live in DeKalb
forever, even if it's not the West,
maybe because I'm writing him
how much I need to stay alive.
I think how Patrick and Paul loved Barney
and will love her even more
through Bootsie when they meet.
Bob loves them all in his rain-in-the-barrel
way, and through Kokomo, his cat,
who keeps napping as if Gene hasn't died.
As if Bob has left Vermont
and is capturing the full moon

over Dodge from a train that keeps trying
the loping rails west.

So I'll visit Alvaro in New Mexico
and not write. A letter, that is,
though I'll still skill the sky.
Because I love him, as I love Gene,
even though Gene's tired of me
disturbing his rest. Though it's eternal,
so one more letter can't mean much.
Maybe I'll write Eric
before seeing Alvaro because Gene loved Eric
too. Even before Gene died.
As he loved my wrist. The one red
with ants swollen in bitten blood.
The blood John sends back to me each day
when he writes to help me somehow stay alive.

WE SLEPT THE ANIMAL

Below Buffalo Willows

Give us a kiss. Goodbye, dear. The buffalo
willows were full of hurt, and then the fire died.
Kiss the neck, the nape, the cheek. Somehow we survive
all the depths of deaths living gifts us. I have cried.
I am not a we, but you are me,
and we are here. Whenever we die. Wherever
we had lived before, with the sheep, the cattle,
all the long grass long as a ribbed rib of sleep.
Yes, there was dust. We slept the animal.
We slipped back and forth many times until
we got it right. The woman the man hoped
to be was scarred. The man she bled, hurt.
Say some touch or other. The way we hold
a hand grieves us tough gusts that beat us
back. A kiss. Give it. Grieve it. Give us a way.
This mouth or that, we are all tick-tonguing
our way around the tree bark of the heart. Say something.
This time. Anything. Nothing would be enough.

NOTES

There are several poems throughout this book written to friends named "John," always identified in the poems' dedications. However, the unidentified "John" who roams in and out of this book, referred to (without a last name) in the following poems, is John Bradley: "Letter to Ray from Livermore," "Letter to Alvaro from San Luis," "Letter to Hugo from Cowdry," "Dead Skunk," "Little Infinite Poem, Or Letter to Bob from Everywhere at Once," and "I'm Writing Gene a Letter," as well as the non-letter poem dedicated to him: "Dejected in Boulder, I Think of James Wright's 'Depressed by a Book of Bad Poetry, I Walk Toward an Unused Pasture and Invite the Insects to Join Me.'"

Epigraphs are from the following:

Richard Hugo (opening epigraph), from *The Lady in Kicking Horse Reservoir*, W.W. Norton & Company, Inc., 1973;

Tom Hennen (opening epigraph), from *Darkness Sticks to Everything*, Copper Canyon Press, 2013;

Craig Courier (in "Colorado Sheep Wars, 1894"), from the September 14, 1894 edition;

Mark H. Brown and W.R. Felton (in "House of Green Buffalo Hides. Slabs of Hump at Right, North Montana, January 1882"), from *The Frontier Years*, Bramball House, 1955;

Miguel Hernández (in "Letter to Alvaro from San Luis"), from *Selected Poems: Miguel Hernández and Blas de Otero*, edited by Timothy Baland and Hardie St. Martin, Beacon Press, 1972;

William Stafford (in "Letter to Bill from Fort Collins [Just Back from Polson]"), from "An Interview with William Stafford" (by George Kalamaras and Mary Ann Cain), *Ground Water Review*, Nos. 1 & 2, Spring 1984;

Oliver Wendell Holmes (in "Letter to Tony from Cheyenne Wells"), from *Ralph Waldo Emerson*, Houghton, Mifflin & Company, 1885.

In "House of Green Buffalo Hides. Slabs of Hump at Right, North Montana, January 1882," the phrases in section one, "A sitting position with rest sticks / was preferred by most" and "*Make the kill / in as small an area as possible*," and the list of supplies in section seven, are adapted from Mark H. Brown and W.R. Felton, *The Frontier Years*, Bramball House, 1955.

In "Letter to Juan from North Platte" and "Letter to Mary from the Snow of Buffalo Bones on the Laramie Plains," the phrase "*exuberant political need to love*" is from César Vallejo, *The Complete Posthumous Poetry*, translated by Clayton Eshleman and José Rubia Barcia, University of California Press, 1978.

In "Letter to Joe from Durango" and "Letter to Michelle from Victor," the phrases, "*crucified to the wheel while she was still beautiful*" and "*He saw the veins of men as a net the gods made to catch us in like wild beasts*," respectively, are from George Seferis, *Collected Poems*, translated by Edmund Keeley and Philip Sherrard, Princeton University Press, 1981.

In "Letter to Robert from Ridgway," the passage, "*Submission is the effort of the inferior to attain friendly or harmonious social integration*," is from Rudolph Schenkel's classic wolf behavior study, quoted in *Wolves: Behavior, Ecology, and Conservation*, edited by L. David Mech and Luigi Boitani, University of Chicago Press, 2003.

"Letter to Phil from Manitou Springs" includes the Wallace Stevens line, "*the ordinary of his commonplace,*" from *The Collected Poems of Wallace Stevens*, Alfred A. Knopf, 1954.

"Letter to Arthur from Ault" includes a quote from the mother of Li Ho, "*My son will not stop until he has vomited up his heart!*" This poem also includes a line from Tu Fu, "*And the war goes on and on,*" also referenced in "Letter to Megan from Rifle," all from *Five T'ang Poets*, translated by David Young, Oberlin College Press, 1990.

"Letter to Don from Gunbarrel" includes a phrase, "When it rains, a certain fish / up the canyon gets its name," an adaptation of something Andrea Rexilius has said.

"Letter to Judy from Colorado Springs" includes the phrases, "*the thin-gummed man*" and "*great angry owl in search of its kill,*" which are from Judith Johnson Sherwin's, *How the Dead Count*, W.W. Norton & Company, Inc., 1978. The lines, "*cities of mathematics*" and "*a poetics of generosity,*" are from one of her book and essay titles, respectively.

"Letter to Reg from Cheyenne" includes the phrase, *scarlet fever, childbirth in a mud box,*" which is drawn from Reg Saner's "Sod Huts on the Plains near Aurora, Colorado," from *Climbing Into the Roots*, Harper & Row, Publishers, 1975. This same poem is referenced in "Letter to Gerrit from Aurora" and "Letter to Tony from Cheyenne Wells."

In "Letter to Eric from Cripple Creek," the quoted passage in stanza two is an approximation of a quote from Swami Kriyananda's audio lectures, *Lessons in Yoga: 14 Steps to Higher Awareness*, Crystal Clarity Publishers, 1989.

In "Letter to John from Denver," references to "a living Batch" quote from and adapt Ed Dorn's passage, "I is now a living Batch," from *Gunslinger: Book II*, Black Sparrow Press, 1969.

"Letter to Larry from Bellvue" includes the passage, "And what of Aimé Césaire. He who Krakatoa. He who everything better than a monsoon?" Part of this is an adaptation of Césaire's lines, "I who Krakatoa / I who everything better than a monsoon," from *Aimé Césaire: The Collected Poetry*, translated by Clayton Eshleman and Annette Smith, University of California Press, 1983.

"Letter to Tremblay from Tie Siding" and "*The Branch Will Not Break*. Letter to Kevin from Livermore" include the passage, "*Time is wider than it is long*," a phrase seemingly coined and often repeated by the extraordinary visual artist and my dear departed friend Gene Hoffman.

"Letter to Sam from Crow Agency" includes the passage, "Say no. You're talking to four storerooms of books," an adaptation of a passage from Richard Hugo's *The Lady in Kicking Horse Reservoir* (cited earlier).

In "*The Branch Will Not Break*. Letter to Kevin from Livermore," there are references to James Wright's poems, "Lying in a Hammock at William Duffy's Farm in Pine Island, Minnesota" and "Northern Pike," from *The Branch Will Not*

Break, Wesleyan University Press, 1963, and *Collected Poems*, Wesleyan University Press, 1971, respectively.

"Little Infinite Poem, Or Letter to Bob from Everywhere at Once" includes "*blind camels of Isfahan*," an adaptation of Philip Appleman's "the blind camel at Isfahan," from *Open Doorways*, W.W. Norton & Company, Inc., 1976, as well as an adaptation of a Federico García Lorca line from "Little Infinite Poem"—"to get down on all fours for twenty centuries and eat the grasses of the cemeteries"—from *Selected Poems of Lorca and Jiménez*, chosen and translated by Robert Bly, Beacon Press, 1973.

In "Letter to Lisa from the In-Between," the name of her glorious German Shepherd, Pharoah, is indeed spelled correctly—mirroring the spelling of the jazz great Pharoah Sanders and not the pharaohs of Egypt.

In "Letter to Tony from Cheyenne Wells," the quote, "*Too much has been made of Emerson's mysticism*," is from Oliver Wendell Holmes, cited earlier.

"Letter to Hugo from Kicking Horse Reservoir" includes the line, "Kicking the gravel / loose as you have," which is a reference to the film, *Richard Hugo: Kicking the Loose Gravel Home*. Produced and directed by Annick Smith. Written and edited by Beth Chadwick Ferris and Annick Smith. Cinematography by Ron Carraher. KUFM-TV Montana PBS/The University of Montana, 1976.

"Letter to Kent from Fort Wayne" includes references to James Wright's poem, "Lying in a Hammock at William Duffy's Farm in Pine Island, Minnesota," from *The Branch*

Will Not Break (cited earlier). The quote in the first three lines comes from Mary Rose O'Reilley's memoir, *The Barn at the End of the World: The Apprenticeship of a Quaker, Buddhist Shepherd*, Milkweed Editions, 2000.

In "Saidshaft. Letter to Mary from Albuquerque," the phrase "Unceasing blessings" is a complimentary closing that was often used by the yogi Paramahansa Yogananda. In my correspondence with Mary, I often used this closing as well; she loved and adopted it during her final months. Thus, I wanted to honor my friend with this phrase—giving it back to her, so to speak—near the closing of this elegy.

The authorship of other occasional quotations in this book should hopefully be clear from the various contexts in which those quotations appear.

ABOUT THE AUTHOR

GEORGE KALAMARAS, former Poet Laureate of Indiana (2014–2016), is the author of ten full-length books of poetry and seven poetry chapbooks. He has received several national prizes for his poetry, and he spent several months in India in 1994 on an Indo-U.S. Advanced Research Fellowship. He is Professor of English at Purdue University Fort Wayne (formerly Indiana University-Purdue University Fort Wayne), where he has taught since 1990. He lives with his wife, writer Mary Ann Cain, and their beagle, Bootsie, in Fort Wayne, Indiana. They regularly return to northern Colorado where George and Mary Ann lived for several years in the 1980s.

OTHER BOOKS BY GEORGE KALAMARAS
PUBLISHED BY DOS MADRES PRESS

LUMINOUS IN THE OWL'S RIB (2019)

FOR THE FULL DOS MADRES PRESS CATALOG:
www.dosmadres.com

www.ingramcontent.com/pod-product-compliance
Lightning Source LLC
Chambersburg PA
CBHW021425070526
44577CB00001B/58